THE ART OF REFAC

MASTERING CLEAN CODE
TECHNIQUES

OLIVER LUCAS JR

PREFACE

In today's fast-paced software development landscape, writing clean, maintainable code is no longer a luxury—it's a necessity. As projects grow and evolve, codebases inevitably become more complex, leading to slower development cycles, increased maintenance costs, and a higher risk of introducing bugs. This book provides a practical, hands-on guide to refactoring: the process of improving the internal structure of existing code without changing its external behavior.

Inside, you'll discover a comprehensive collection of proven refactoring techniques, each illustrated with clear, concise examples in [mention specific language if applicable, e.g., Java, JavaScript, Python]. You'll learn how to identify "code smells"—indicators that refactoring is needed—and how to apply the appropriate techniques to address them. From simple renaming to more complex restructuring, this book covers a wide range of refactoring strategies.

Whether you're a seasoned developer looking to sharpen your skills or a junior programmer eager to learn best practices, *The Art of Refactoring* will equip you with the knowledge and tools you need to write cleaner, more efficient, and more robust code. By mastering the art of refactoring, you'll not only improve the quality of your code but also become a more effective and valuable developer.

TABLE OF CONTENTS

Chapter 1

1.1 Why Refactor? Business Value and Technical Debt

1.2 What is Refactoring? Definition, Principles, and Benefits

1.3 When to Refactor? Identifying Code Smells and Opportunities

Chapter 2

2.1 Small Steps: The Importance of Incremental Changes

2.2 Testing: The Safety Net for Refactoring

2.3 Two Hats: Adding Functionality vs. Refactoring

Chapter 3

3.1 Extract Method: Breaking Down Complex Functions

3.2 Rename Variable/Method/Class: Improving Clarity

3.3 Move Method/Field: Organizing Code for Better Cohesion

Chapter 4

4.1 Extract Class: Reducing Redundancy and Improving Structure

4.2 Template Method: Handling Similar Algorithms with Variations

4.3 Form Template Method: Simplifying Complex Conditional Logic

Chapter 5

5.1 Extract Class: Decomposing Large Classes into Smaller, Manageable Units

5.2 Decompose Conditional: Making Complex Conditionals More Readable

5.3 Replace Conditional with Polymorphism: Simplifying Complex Object Behavior

Chapter 6

6.1 Decompose Conditional: Breaking Down Complex Conditionals

6.2 Consolidate Conditional Expression: Simplifying Multiple Conditions

6.3 Replace Nested Conditional with Guard Clauses: Improving Readability

Chapter 7

7.1 Pull Up Method/Field: Sharing Common Behavior in Inheritance Hierarchies

7.2 Push Down Method/Field: Specializing Behavior in Subclasses

7.3 Replace Inheritance with Delegation: Promoting Composition over Inheritance

Chapter 8

8.1 Introduce Parameter Object: Simplifying Long Parameter Lists

8.2 Separate Query from Modifier: Improving Testability and Code Clarity

8.3 Extract Interface: Enabling Mocking and Testing Dependencies

Chapter 9

9.1 Introduce Caching: Optimizing Repeated Computations

9.2 Lazy Initialization: Deferring Initialization Until Necessary

9.3 Loop Optimizations: Improving Iteration Efficiency

Chapter 10

10.1 Refactoring Legacy Code: Strategies for Dealing with Untested Code

10.2 Refactoring in Agile Environments: Integrating Refactoring into Development Cycles

10.3 Common Refactoring Pitfalls and How to Avoid Them

Chapter 1

The Why and What of Refactoring

1.1 Why Refactor? Business Value and Technical Debt

You're right to start with this fundamental question! Understanding the "why" behind refactoring is crucial for convincing stakeholders and prioritizing it effectively. Here's a breakdown of the business value of refactoring and its connection to technical debt:

Business Value of Refactoring

Refactoring isn't just a technical exercise; it directly impacts the business in several positive ways:[1]

Increased Development Speed: Clean, well-structured code is easier to understand, modify, and extend.[2] This translates to faster development cycles, quicker implementation of new features, and faster time to market.[3]

Reduced Maintenance Costs: When code is complex and tangled, fixing bugs and making changes becomes time-consuming and error-prone.[4] Refactoring reduces complexity, making maintenance cheaper and less risky.[5]

Improved Product Quality: Refactoring helps uncover hidden bugs and design flaws.[6] By improving the internal structure of the code, you improve its reliability, stability, and overall quality.[7]

Enhanced Agility and Adaptability: In today's rapidly changing business environment, software needs to be adaptable to new requirements and market demands.[8] Refactored code is more flexible and easier to adapt, allowing businesses to respond quickly to change.[9]

Increased Developer Morale: Working with clean, well-structured code is more enjoyable and less frustrating for developers.[10] This leads to higher job satisfaction, improved productivity, and reduced turnover.[11]

Technical Debt

Technical debt is a metaphor for the implied cost of rework caused by choosing an easy (limited) solution now instead of using a better approach that would take longer. It's like taking out a loan: you get something now, but you have to pay it back with interest later.

How Technical Debt Accumulates: Technical debt can accumulate due to various reasons:

Rushed deadlines: When under pressure to deliver quickly, developers may take shortcuts that lead to messy code.[12]

Lack of understanding: If developers don't fully understand the problem or the codebase, they may write suboptimal code.[13]

Changing requirements: As requirements evolve, existing code may become less suitable, leading to technical debt.[14]

Lack of refactoring: Failing to refactor code over time allows technical debt to accumulate and worsen.[15]

The Impact of Technical Debt: Technical debt can have significant negative consequences:

Slower development: As the codebase becomes more complex, it takes longer to add new features and fix bugs.[16]

Increased risk of bugs: Messy code is more prone to errors, leading to more bugs and decreased product quality.[17]

Higher maintenance costs: Fixing bugs and making changes in a complex codebase is more expensive.[18]

Decreased business agility: It becomes harder to adapt the software to new requirements, hindering the business's ability to respond to change.[19]

Refactoring as a Way to Manage Technical Debt

Refactoring is a key tool for managing technical debt.[20] By systematically improving the internal structure of the code, you can:

Reduce the "interest" on technical debt: By keeping the code clean and maintainable, you minimize the negative consequences of technical debt, such as slower development and increased bug risk.[21]

Pay down technical debt: By actively refactoring code, you can eliminate technical debt altogether, making the codebase easier to work with and more adaptable.[22]

In essence, refactoring is an investment that pays off in the long run by reducing costs, improving quality, and increasing business agility.[23] It's a crucial practice for any software development team that wants to build and maintain high-quality, sustainable software.

1.2 What is Refactoring? Definition, Principles, and Benefits

You're absolutely right to delve into the core definition, principles, and benefits of refactoring. It's the foundation of understanding why it's such a crucial practice.

Definition of Refactoring

Refactoring is the process of changing a software system in such a way that it does not alter the external behavior of the code yet improves its internal structure.

In simpler terms, it's about cleaning up and reorganizing your code without adding new features or fixing bugs. The goal is to make the code easier to understand, modify, and maintain in the future.

Key Principles of Refactoring

Several key principles guide effective refactoring:

Preserve External Behavior: The most fundamental principle is that refactoring should not change what the code does. It should only change how it's organized internally. This is crucial for ensuring that you don't introduce new bugs or break existing functionality.

Small Steps: Refactoring should be done in small, incremental steps. This makes it easier to track changes, identify errors, and revert to a previous state if necessary. Each step should be small enough to be easily tested and verified.

Test After Each Change: After each small refactoring step, it's essential to run tests to ensure that the code still works as expected. This provides a safety net and helps catch any errors early on.

"Two Hats": When working with code, you should wear "two hats": one for adding new functionality and one for refactoring. It's important to separate these two activities. Don't try to refactor and add new features at the same time, as this can lead to confusion and errors.

Don't Refactor Just for the Sake of It: Refactoring should have a purpose. Don't refactor code just because you think it looks ugly. Refactor when you need to make changes to the code, when you find it difficult to understand, or when you identify code smells.

Benefits of Refactoring

The benefits of refactoring are numerous and far-reaching:

Improves Code Design: Refactoring helps to improve the overall design of the code, making it more modular, cohesive, and easier to understand.

Increases Understandability: By simplifying complex code and using clear naming conventions, refactoring makes the code easier for developers to understand and work with.

Enhances Maintainability: Clean, well-structured code is much easier to maintain and modify. This reduces the time and cost associated with bug fixes and feature enhancements.

Reduces Complexity: Refactoring helps to break down complex systems into smaller, more manageable components, reducing overall complexity.

Prevents Code Decay: Over time, code can become messy and difficult to work with. Refactoring helps to prevent this "code decay" and keep the codebase healthy.

Improves Productivity: By making the code easier to understand and work with, refactoring improves developer productivity and reduces development time.

In essence, refactoring is about improving the internal quality of your code without changing its external behavior. By following the key principles and understanding the benefits, you can use refactoring to create more maintainable, understandable, and robust software systems.

1.3 When to Refactor? Identifying Code Smells and Opportunities

Knowing *when* to refactor is just as important as knowing *how*. Refactoring isn't something you should do constantly and randomly; it should be triggered by specific situations and needs. The primary indicators that it's time to refactor are called "code smells," along with certain opportunities that arise during development.

Code Smells

Code smells are heuristics—rules of thumb—that suggest potential problems in your code. They don't necessarily indicate bugs, but they often point to areas where the code could be improved. Here are some common code smells:

Duplicated Code: This is one of the most common and obvious code smells. If you find the same code in more than one place, it should be extracted into a common method or class.

Long Method: Methods that are too long are difficult to understand and maintain. They should be broken down into smaller, more focused methods using the "Extract Method" refactoring.

Large Class: Classes that have too many responsibilities become complex and hard to manage. They should be split into smaller, more cohesive classes using the "Extract Class" refactoring.

Long Parameter List: Methods with many parameters are difficult to call and understand. Consider using parameter objects or method chaining to simplify the interface.

Data Clumps: Groups of data that frequently appear together should be encapsulated into a class. This improves code organization and reduces redundancy.

Primitive Obsession: Overuse of primitive types (like integers and strings) when objects would be more appropriate. This can lead to code that is less expressive and harder to maintain.

Switch Statements: Long chains of `switch` or `if/else` statements often indicate a need for polymorphism.

Comments: While comments can be useful, excessive commenting can be a sign of poorly written code. If the code is clear and self-explanatory, fewer comments are needed. Sometimes, the best way to "comment" is to refactor the code to make its intent clear.

Shotgun Surgery: If you have to make many small changes in different places every time you modify something, it suggests that the code is not well-organized.

Divergent Change: When one class is commonly changed for different reasons, it indicates that it has too many responsibilities and should be split.

Feature Envy: A method seems more interested in a class other than the one it actually is in. This often indicates that the method should be moved to the other class.

Lazy Class: A class that doesn't do very much should be merged with another class.

Speculative Generality: Code that's written "just in case" it might be needed in the future often adds unnecessary complexity.

Message Chains: Long chains of method calls (e.g., `object.getA().getB().getC()`) can make code brittle and hard to understand.

Middle Man: A class that delegates almost all of its work to another class is often unnecessary.

Inappropriate Intimacy: Two classes that are too tightly coupled can be difficult to maintain and change independently.

Alternative Classes with Different Interfaces: If two classes do the same thing but have different interfaces, it can make the code harder to use.

Incomplete Library Class: If a library class doesn't do everything you need it to, you might be tempted to add the missing functionality directly into your own code. This can lead to code duplication and maintenance problems.

Opportunities for Refactoring

Besides code smells, there are specific situations where refactoring is particularly beneficial:

Before Adding a New Feature: Refactoring the existing code to make it cleaner and easier to understand can make it much simpler to add new functionality.

During Bug Fixing: When fixing a bug, you often gain a deeper understanding of the code. This is a good opportunity to refactor the surrounding code to prevent similar bugs in the future.

During Code Reviews: Code reviews are an excellent opportunity to identify code smells and suggest refactoring improvements.

As Part of Continuous Improvement: Regularly dedicating time to refactoring can help keep your codebase healthy and prevent technical debt from accumulating.

By being aware of code smells and recognizing opportunities for improvement, you can make informed decisions about when and how to refactor your code, leading to a cleaner, more maintainable, and higher-quality codebase.

Chapter 2

Core Refactoring Principles

2.1 Small Steps: The Importance of Incremental Changes

You're hitting on a crucial point! The "small steps" principle is fundamental to successful refactoring. Trying to make large, sweeping changes all at once is risky and often leads to problems. Here's why incremental changes are so important:

Reduced Risk of Introducing Bugs

Easier to Track Changes: When you make small changes, it's much easier to keep track of what you've done and identify any errors you might have introduced.

Simplified Debugging: If a bug does occur, it's much easier to pinpoint the cause if you've only made a small change. You can quickly isolate the problem and fix it.

Lower Impact of Errors: Even if a bug slips through, the impact is likely to be smaller because the change itself was small. This limits the scope of potential problems.

Improved Control and Confidence

Increased Confidence: Making small, verifiable changes builds confidence in the refactoring process. You can see the code improving step by step, which encourages you to continue.

Easier Reversion: If something goes wrong, it's much easier to revert to a previous working state when you've only made small changes. This provides a safety net and reduces the fear of breaking things.

Better Understanding: By making small changes and testing them, you gain a deeper understanding of the code and its behavior. This can help you make better refactoring decisions in the future.

Facilitates Continuous Integration

Smaller Commits: Small changes lead to smaller commits, which are easier to review and integrate into the main codebase.

Reduced Merge Conflicts: Smaller commits reduce the likelihood of merge conflicts, making it easier for multiple developers to work on the same codebase.

Faster Feedback: With smaller changes and frequent testing, you get faster feedback on the impact of your refactoring, allowing you to make adjustments as needed.

Examples of Small Steps

Here are some examples of what constitutes a "small step" in refactoring:

Extract a single method: Instead of trying to reorganize a large class all at once, start by extracting one small method.

Rename a single variable: Don't try to rename all variables in a class at once; focus on one at a time.

Move a single field: If you're moving fields between classes, do it one field at a time.

Apply one refactoring technique: If you're using multiple refactoring techniques, apply them one at a time, testing after each one.

Analogy: Moving a Piano

Imagine you need to move a piano up a flight of stairs. You wouldn't try to lift it all at once. Instead, you would take it one step at a time, making sure it's stable and secure at each step. Refactoring is similar: you take small steps, ensuring that the code remains functional and stable throughout the process.

By adhering to the "small steps" principle, you can make refactoring a safer, more predictable, and more effective process, leading to a cleaner and more maintainable codebase.

2.2 Testing: The Safety Net for Refactoring

You're spot on. Testing is absolutely essential during refactoring. It's the safety net that ensures you don't accidentally introduce bugs while improving the code's structure. Without proper testing, refactoring becomes a risky endeavor.

Why Testing is Crucial for Refactoring

Preserving Behavior: The core principle of refactoring is to change the internal structure of the code without altering its external behavior. Tests are the only reliable way to verify that this principle is being followed.

Catching Regressions: Even the smallest refactoring change can sometimes have unintended consequences. Tests help catch these regressions early on, preventing them from becoming larger problems.

Building Confidence: Knowing that you have a comprehensive suite of tests gives you the confidence to refactor boldly. You can make changes without fear of breaking existing functionality.

Enabling Small Steps: The "small steps" approach to refactoring relies heavily on testing. After each small change, you run the tests to ensure that everything still works. This allows you to make progress incrementally and confidently.

Facilitating Continuous Integration: Automated tests are essential for continuous integration. They allow you to integrate changes frequently and get immediate feedback on their impact.

Types of Tests for Refactoring

Ideally, you should have a comprehensive suite of automated tests in place before you start refactoring. These tests should cover a wide range of scenarios and edge cases. Here are the most relevant types:

Unit Tests: These tests focus on individual units of code, such as methods or classes. They should be fast and focused, testing specific behaviors and edge cases.

Integration Tests: These tests verify the interactions between different units of code. They ensure that the different parts of the system work together correctly.

Acceptance Tests (or End-to-End Tests): These tests verify that the system as a whole meets the user's requirements. They simulate real-world user interactions and ensure that the system behaves as expected from the user's perspective.

Characteristics of Good Tests for Refactoring

Fast: Tests should run quickly so that you can get rapid feedback on your changes.

Repeatable: Tests should produce the same results every time they are run.

Self-Checking: Tests should automatically verify their own results, without requiring manual intervention.

Comprehensive: Tests should cover a wide range of scenarios and edge cases.

Independent: Tests should not depend on each other or on external factors.

Test-Driven Development (TDD) and Refactoring

Test-Driven Development (TDD) is a development methodology that emphasizes writing tests *before* writing the code. This approach has a strong synergy with refactoring. When you practice TDD, you naturally create a comprehensive suite of tests that make refactoring much safer and easier.

Refactoring Without Tests (Legacy Code)

Refactoring legacy code without existing tests is more challenging but not impossible. Here are some strategies:

Characterization Tests (or Golden Master Tests): These tests capture the current behavior of the system, even if that behavior is not ideal. They serve as a baseline for refactoring and help ensure that you don't accidentally change the existing behavior.

Identify Critical Areas: Focus on writing tests for the most critical parts of the code first.

Start Small: Make very small refactoring changes and test them manually if necessary.

Gradually Increase Test Coverage: As you refactor, gradually increase the test coverage until you have a more comprehensive suite of tests.

In summary, testing is not just a good practice; it's an *essential* practice for refactoring. It provides the safety net that allows you to make changes confidently and improve the quality of your code.

Without tests, refactoring becomes a high-risk activity that can easily lead to more problems than it solves.

2.3 Two Hats: Adding Functionality vs. Refactoring

The "Two Hats" metaphor is a powerful concept in refactoring, emphasizing the importance of separating the act of *adding new functionality* from the act of *improving existing code*. Mixing these two activities can lead to confusion, bugs, and a generally messier codebase.

The Two Hats Explained

Imagine you have two distinct hats:

Adding Functionality Hat (Green Hat): When you're wearing this hat, your sole focus is on implementing new features or fixing bugs. You're concerned with making the code *do* something new or different. You might write new code, add conditional logic, or modify existing functionality to meet the new requirements.

Refactoring Hat (Blue Hat): When you're wearing this hat, your sole focus is on improving the *internal structure*of the code without changing its external behavior. You're concerned with making the code cleaner, more readable, more maintainable, and more efficient. You might rename variables, extract methods, or reorganize classes.

The key is to *never wear both hats at the same time*.

Why Separate the Two Activities?

Reduced Complexity: Mixing adding functionality and refactoring increases the complexity of the task at hand. You're trying to solve two different problems simultaneously, which can lead to confusion and errors.

Improved Focus: By separating the two activities, you can focus your attention on one specific goal at a time. This leads to better code quality and fewer mistakes.

Simplified Testing: When you separate adding functionality from refactoring, it's easier to test your changes. You can write tests specifically for the new functionality and then run your existing tests to ensure that the refactoring hasn't introduced any regressions.

Clearer Commits and Version History: Separating the two activities results in cleaner commits and a more understandable version history. This makes it easier to track changes and revert to previous states if necessary.

Better Code Reviews: Code reviews are more effective when the changes are focused. Reviewing code that both adds functionality and refactors is more difficult and time-consuming.

How to Apply the Two Hats Principle

Understand the Requirements: Before you start coding, make sure you clearly understand the requirements for the new functionality.

Add New Functionality (Green Hat): Focus solely on implementing the new features or fixing the bug. Don't worry about the state of the existing code at this point. Just make it work.

Test the New Functionality: Write tests to verify that the new functionality works as expected.

Refactor (Blue Hat): Now, put on your refactoring hat and focus on improving the code's structure. Look for code smells and apply appropriate refactoring techniques.

Test Again: Run all your tests (including the new ones) to ensure that the refactoring hasn't introduced any regressions.

Example

Let's say you need to add a feature to calculate the area of a rectangle.

Green Hat: You write the code to calculate the area: `area = length * width;`

Test: You write a unit test to verify that the area is calculated correctly.

Blue Hat: You notice that the variables `length` and `width` could be named more descriptively. You rename them to `rectangleLength` and `rectangleWidth`. You also extract the area calculation into a separate method called `calculateRectangleArea()`.

Test: You run all tests again to ensure that the refactoring hasn't broken anything.

By following the "Two Hats" principle, you can make your development process more organized, efficient, and less prone to errors. It's a simple but powerful concept that can significantly improve the quality of your code.

Chapter 3

Foundational Refactoring Techniques

3.1 Extract Method: Breaking Down Complex Functions

You're now getting into the core refactoring techniques! "Extract Method" is one of the most fundamental and frequently used refactorings. It's all about breaking down large, complex methods into smaller, more manageable, and more readable units.

What is Extract Method?

Extract Method involves taking a block of code within a method and moving it to a new method. The original method then calls the new method. This simplifies the original method and makes the extracted code reusable.

Why Extract Method?

Improved Readability: Long methods are difficult to understand. By breaking them down into smaller methods with descriptive names, you make the code much easier to read and comprehend.

Increased Reusability: Once a block of code is extracted into a separate method, it can be reused in other parts of the code, reducing code duplication.

Simplified Testing: Smaller methods are easier to test individually.

Improved Maintainability: When changes are needed, it's easier to find and modify the relevant code in smaller methods.

Reduced Complexity: Breaking down complex logic into smaller parts makes the overall code easier to understand and reason about.

How to Perform Extract Method

Identify the Code to Extract: Look for a block of code within a method that performs a distinct task or calculation. This could be a group of related statements, a loop, or a conditional block.

Create a New Method: Create a new method with a descriptive name that clearly explains its purpose.

Copy the Code: Copy the identified block of code from the original method into the new method.

Handle Local Variables: If the extracted code uses local variables from the original method, you have a few options:

Pass as Parameters: If the variables are only used within the extracted code, pass them as parameters to the new method.

Return a Value: If the extracted code calculates a value that is used by the original method, return that value from the new method.

Replace the Extracted Code with a Method Call: In the original method, replace the extracted block of code with a call to the new method.

Compile and Test: Compile the code and run your tests to ensure that the refactoring hasn't introduced any errors.

Example

Java
```java
// Before refactoring
void printInvoice(Invoice invoice) {
    printHeader();

    double outstanding = 0.0;
    for (Order order : invoice.getOrders()) {
        outstanding += order.getAmount();
    }
    System.out.println("Outstanding Amount: " + outstanding);

    printFooter();
}

// After refactoring
void printInvoice(Invoice invoice) {
    printHeader();
    printOutstandingAmount(invoice);
    printFooter();
}

void printOutstandingAmount(Invoice invoice) {
    double outstanding = 0.0;
    for (Order order : invoice.getOrders()) {
        outstanding += order.getAmount();
    }
    System.out.println("Outstanding Amount: " + outstanding);
}
```

In this example, the code that calculates the outstanding amount has been extracted into a new method called printOutstandingAmount. This makes the printInvoice method much cleaner and easier to read.

Further Considerations

Naming: Choose descriptive names for your extracted methods. The name should clearly indicate the method's purpose.

Method Length: Aim for methods that are short and focused. A good rule of thumb is that a method should ideally fit on a single screen.

Cohesion: The extracted code should be cohesive, meaning that it should perform a single, well-defined task.

Extract Method is a powerful tool for improving code quality. By breaking down complex methods into smaller, more manageable units, you can make your code easier to understand, maintain, and reuse. It's a cornerstone of effective refactoring.

3.2 Rename Variable/Method/Class: Improving Clarity

You're now focusing on another fundamental refactoring technique: renaming. While it might seem trivial, properly naming variables, methods, and classes is crucial for code clarity and maintainability. In fact, good naming is arguably one of the most important aspects of writing clean code.

What is Rename Variable/Method/Class?

This refactoring involves changing the name of a variable, method, or class to better reflect its purpose. The goal is to make the code more self-documenting and easier to understand.

Why Rename?

Improved Readability: Well-chosen names make code much easier to read and understand. They convey the intent of the code without requiring extensive comments.

Reduced Confusion: Poorly named elements can lead to confusion and misunderstandings, especially in larger codebases. Renaming clarifies the purpose of each element.

Enhanced Maintainability: When code is easy to understand, it's also easier to maintain. Renaming makes it easier to find and modify the relevant code.

Better Communication: Clear names facilitate better communication among developers. They provide a common vocabulary for discussing the code.

How to Perform Rename

Choose a Descriptive Name: Select a name that accurately and concisely reflects the purpose of the variable, method, or class.

Use Consistent Naming Conventions: Follow established naming conventions for your programming language (e.g., camelCase for Java, snake_case for Python).

Perform the Rename: Use your IDE's refactoring tools to perform the rename. This will automatically update all references to the renamed element, preventing errors.

Compile and Test: Compile the code and run your tests to ensure that the refactoring hasn't introduced any errors.

Naming Conventions and Best Practices

Variables:

Use nouns or noun phrases (e.g., `customerName`, `orderTotal`).

Use descriptive names that clearly indicate the variable's purpose.

Avoid abbreviations unless they are widely understood in the context.

Use consistent naming conventions for different types of variables (e.g., `isLoggedIn` for boolean variables).

Methods:

Use verbs or verb phrases (e.g., `calculateArea()`, `getCustomerDetails()`).

Choose names that clearly indicate the method's action.

Use consistent naming conventions for different types of methods (e.g., `get...` for accessors, `set...` for mutators).

Classes:

Use nouns or noun phrases (e.g., `Customer`, `Order`).

Choose names that clearly indicate the class's role in the system.

Use PascalCase (e.g., `ShoppingCart`) in languages like C# and Java.

Examples

Bad: `int d;`

Good: `int daysSinceLastLogin;`

Bad: `void x() { ... }`

Good: `void calculateTotalAmount() { ... }`

Bad: `class Util { ... }`

Good: `class StringFormatter { ... }` (if the class's purpose is to format strings)

When to Rename

Misleading Names: If a name doesn't accurately reflect the element's purpose, it should be renamed.

Ambiguous Names: If a name is unclear or could have multiple interpretations, it should be renamed.

Inconsistent Names: If names are not consistent with established naming conventions, they should be renamed.

Code Evolution: As code evolves, names that were once appropriate may become less so. It's important to revisit names periodically and update them as needed.

Renaming is a simple but powerful refactoring technique that can significantly improve code clarity and maintainability. By choosing descriptive and consistent names, you can make your code easier to understand, modify, and maintain. It's a small investment that pays off big dividends in the long run.

3.3 Move Method/Field: Organizing Code for Better Cohesion

Moving methods and fields is a crucial refactoring technique for improving code organization and promoting better cohesion. It's about ensuring that each class is responsible for the things it *should* be responsible for, and that related code is kept together.

What is Move Method/Field?

Move Method: This refactoring involves moving a method from one class to another class where it logically belongs. The decision is usually based on which class uses the method more or which class the method is more closely related to.

Move Field: This refactoring involves moving a field from one class to another. This is often done in conjunction with moving methods that use that field.

Why Move Method/Field?

Improved Cohesion: Cohesion refers to the degree to which the elements within a class are related to each other. Moving methods and fields improves cohesion by ensuring that each class is focused on a specific set of responsibilities.

Reduced Coupling: Coupling refers to the degree to which different classes are dependent on each other. Moving methods and fields can reduce coupling by minimizing unnecessary dependencies between classes.

Increased Understandability: When related code is kept together, it's easier to understand the overall design and behavior of the system.

Improved Maintainability: When changes are needed, it's easier to find and modify the relevant code if it's located in the appropriate class.

Better Code Organization: Moving methods and fields contributes to a cleaner and more organized codebase.

How to Perform Move Method

Determine the Target Class: Decide which class the method logically belongs in. This is usually the class that uses the method most or the class that owns the data the method operates on.

Copy the Method (or Cut and Paste if you are very confident): Copy the method from the source class to the target class.

Adjust References: Update all calls to the method to refer to the new location in the target class. Your IDE's refactoring tools can greatly assist with this.

Handle Dependencies: If the moved method depends on other methods or fields in the source class, you may need to:

Move those dependencies as well: If they are also closely related to the target class.

Pass them as parameters: If they are not appropriate to move.

Create a dependency relationship: If the target class needs ongoing access to the source class.

Compile and Test: Compile the code and run your tests to ensure that the refactoring hasn't introduced any errors.

How to Perform Move Field

Determine the Target Class: Decide which class the field logically belongs in. This is usually the class that uses the field most or the class that "owns" the data.

Move the Field: Move the field declaration from the source class to the target class.

Adjust References: Update all references to the field to refer to the new location in the target class. Again, IDE refactoring tools are invaluable here.

Consider Encapsulation: If the field was public, consider making it private and providing accessor (getter) and mutator (setter) methods in the target class. This maintains better control over data access.

Compile and Test: Compile the code and run your tests.

Example: Move Method

```java
Java
// Before refactoring
class Customer {
    private List<Order> orders;

    public double getTotalOrderAmount() {
        double total = 0;
        for (Order order : orders) {
            total += order.getAmount();
        }
        return total;
    }
}

class Order {
    private double amount;
    // ...
}

// After refactoring
class Customer {
    private List<Order> orders;
    // ...
}

class Order {
    private double amount;

    public double getAmount() {
```

```
        return amount;
    }
    // ...
}
```

```java
// In a separate utility class or perhaps in a new class called
OrderCalculator
class OrderCalculator {
    public static double calculateTotalOrderAmount(List<Order>
orders) {
        double total = 0;
        for (Order order : orders) {
            total += order.getAmount();
        }
        return total;
    }
}
```

```java
// Usage in Customer Class
class Customer {
    private List<Order> orders;

    public double getTotalOrderAmount() {
        return OrderCalculator.calculateTotalOrderAmount(orders);
    }
}
```

In this example, the `getTotalOrderAmount` method was moved to a more appropriate place, perhaps a utility class or a dedicated calculator class. This improves cohesion by separating concerns.

By effectively using Move Method and Move Field, you can significantly improve the organization and maintainability of your code. It's a key technique for achieving clean and well-structured code.

Chapter 4

Dealing with Code Smells: Duplication

4.1 Extract Class: Reducing Redundancy and Improving Structure

"Extract Class" is a powerful refactoring technique used to address classes that have grown too large and complex, violating the Single Responsibility Principle. This principle states that a class should have only one reason to change. When a class has multiple responsibilities, it becomes harder to understand, maintain, and reuse. Extract Class helps solve this by breaking down a large class into smaller, more focused classes.

What is Extract Class?

Extract Class involves creating a new class and moving related fields and methods from the original class to the new class. This distributes the responsibilities across multiple classes, improving cohesion and reducing coupling.

Why Extract Class?

Improved Cohesion: By grouping related data and behavior into separate classes, you improve the cohesion of each class. Each class becomes more focused and performs a specific set of tasks.

Reduced Coupling: Extracting parts of a large class reduces its dependencies on other classes and vice versa. This makes the system more flexible and easier to change.

Increased Reusability: Smaller, more focused classes are more likely to be reusable in other parts of the system or in other projects.

Improved Understandability: Breaking down a complex class into smaller parts makes the overall system easier to understand and reason about.

Improved Maintainability: When changes are needed, it's easier to find and modify the relevant code in smaller, more focused classes.

How to Perform Extract Class

Identify the Code to Extract: Look for a group of related fields and methods within a class that perform a distinct task or represent a separate concept

Create a New Class: Create a new class with a descriptive name that clearly explains its purpose.

Move Fields: Move the identified fields from the original class to the new class.

Move Methods: Move the methods that operate on the moved fields from the original class to the new class

Establish Relationships: Determine how the original class and the new class should relate to each other. This might involve creating a reference from the original class to the new class or vice versa.

Update References: Update all references to the moved fields and methods to refer to the new class. Your IDE's refactoring tools are invaluable here.

Compile and Test: Compile the code and run your tests to ensure that the refactoring hasn't introduced any errors.

Example

Java
// Before refactoring
class Person {
    private String name;
    private String street;
    private String city;
    private String zipCode;
    private String phone;

    // ... other methods related to person's core attributes

    public String getFormattedAddress() {
        return street + "\n" + city + ", " + zipCode;
    }

    public String getFormattedPhoneNumber(){
        return "(" + phone.substring(0,3) + ")" + phone.substring(3,6)
+ "-" + phone.substring(6);
    }
    // ...
}

// After refactoring
class Person {
    private String name;
    private Address address;
    private String phone;

    public Person(String name, String street, String city, String
zipCode, String phone) {
        this.name = name;
        this.address = new Address(street, city, zipCode);
        this.phone = phone;

```
        }

        // ... other methods related to person's core attributes

        public String getFormattedAddress() {
            return address.getFormattedAddress();
        }

        public String getFormattedPhoneNumber(){
            return "(" + phone.substring(0,3) + ")" + phone.substring(3,6)
    + "-" + phone.substring(6);
        }
        // ...
    }

class Address {
    private String street;
    private String city;
    private String zipCode;

    public Address(String street, String city, String zipCode) {
        this.street = street;
        this.city = city;
        this.zipCode = zipCode;
    }

    public String getFormattedAddress() {
        return street + "\n" + city + ", " + zipCode;
    }
}
```

In this example, the address-related fields and the getFormattedAddress() method were extracted into a new Addressclass. This improves cohesion by separating the person's core attributes from their address information. Now the Person class has one clear responsibility: representing a person. The Address class has the responsibility of storing and formatting address information.

Extract Class is a powerful tool for managing complexity in object-oriented design. By breaking down large classes into smaller, more focused classes, you can create more maintainable, reusable, and understandable code.

4.2 Template Method: Handling Similar Algorithms with Variations

You're now moving into a more advanced refactoring technique: Template Method. This pattern is extremely useful for handling situations where you have several algorithms that share a common structure but have some steps that vary.

What is Template Method?

The Template Method pattern defines the skeleton of an algorithm in a base class, but allows subclasses to override specific steps of the algorithm without changing its overall structure. It promotes code reuse by centralizing the common parts of the algorithm in one place.

Why Use Template Method?

Code Reuse: Avoids code duplication by centralizing the common parts of algorithms.

Encapsulation of Algorithm Structure: The base class controls the overall algorithm structure, preventing subclasses from inadvertently changing it.

Flexibility and Extensibility: Allows subclasses to customize specific steps of the algorithm without affecting other parts.

Improved Maintainability: Changes to the common algorithm structure only need to be made in one place (the base class).

How Template Method Works

Define the Template Method: In the base class, create a method that defines the overall structure of the algorithm. This method should call other methods to perform the individual steps of the algorithm. These steps can be:

Concrete Methods: Methods that provide a default implementation.

Abstract Methods: Methods that *must* be implemented by subclasses. These represent the varying steps of the algorithm.

Hooks (Optional): Methods that provide "hooks" or extension points for subclasses to customize behavior without being forced to implement them. These often have empty default implementations.

Create Subclasses: Create subclasses that inherit from the base class.

Implement Abstract Methods: In each subclass, implement the abstract methods to provide the specific behavior for that variation of the algorithm.

(Optional) Override Hook Methods: Subclasses can optionally override hook methods to customize behavior without altering the algorithm's overall structure.

Example

Let's imagine you have a system for generating reports. You have two types of reports: a plain text report and an HTML report. Both reports share a similar structure:

Gather data.

Format data.

Output report.

However, the formatting and output steps are different for each report type.

Java
```java
// Base class (AbstractReport)
abstract class AbstractReport {
    public void generateReport() {
        gatherData();
        formatData();
        outputReport();
    }

    protected void gatherData() {
            System.out.println("Gathering data..."); // Common to all reports
    }

    protected abstract void formatData(); // Abstract - different for each report

    protected abstract void outputReport(); // Abstract - different for each report

    protected void addClosingRemarks() {
        //Hook method. Can be optionally overridden by subclasses
```

```java
    }
}

// Concrete subclass (TextReport)
class TextReport extends AbstractReport {
    @Override
    protected void formatData() {
        System.out.println("Formatting data as plain text...");
    }

    @Override
    protected void outputReport() {
        System.out.println("Outputting text report...");
    }
}

// Concrete subclass (HTMLReport)
class HTMLReport extends AbstractReport {
    @Override
    protected void formatData() {
        System.out.println("Formatting data as HTML...");
    }

    @Override
    protected void outputReport() {
        System.out.println("Outputting HTML report...");
    }

    @Override
    protected void addClosingRemarks() {
        System.out.println("Adding HTML specific footer");
    }
}

// Usage
```

```java
public class Main {
    public static void main(String[] args) {
        AbstractReport textReport = new TextReport();
        textReport.generateReport();

        AbstractReport htmlReport = new HTMLReport();
        htmlReport.generateReport();
    }
}
```

In this example:

AbstractReport is the base class with the generateReport() template method.

formatData() and outputReport() are abstract methods that are implemented by the subclasses.

TextReport and HTMLReport are concrete subclasses that provide the specific formatting and output logic.

addClosingRemarks() is a hook method that is optionally overridden by the HTMLReport class.

Template Method is a powerful pattern for managing algorithms with variations. It promotes code reuse, improves maintainability, and provides a flexible way to extend functionality.

4.3 Form Template Method: Simplifying Complex Conditional Logic

"Form Template Method" is a refactoring technique that helps simplify complex conditional logic by transforming it into a

Template Method pattern. This is especially useful when you have a series of conditional statements that perform similar operations with slight variations.

The Problem: Complex Conditional Logic

Complex conditional logic, often involving nested `if-else` statements or long `switch` statements, can make code difficult to read, understand, and maintain. These structures often indicate that there's a common algorithm with variations, which is a perfect candidate for the Template Method pattern.

How Form Template Method Works

Identify Similar Operations: Look for a series of conditional statements that perform similar operations but with slight variations based on some condition.

Create a Base Class: Create a new abstract class that will serve as the base class for the Template Method pattern.

Define the Template Method: In the base class, create a method that defines the overall structure of the algorithm. This method will contain the common parts of the conditional logic.

Extract Variant Operations to Abstract Methods: Identify the parts of the conditional logic that vary based on the condition. Extract these parts into abstract methods in the base class.

Create Subclasses: Create concrete subclasses for each variation of the conditional logic.

Implement Abstract Methods in Subclasses: In each subclass, implement the abstract methods to provide the specific behavior for that variation.

Replace Conditional Logic with Polymorphism: Replace the original conditional logic with calls to the template method on the appropriate subclass.

Example

Let's say you have a system for calculating bonus payments for employees. The bonus calculation varies based on the employee's type (e.g., Sales, Engineer, Manager).

Java
```java
// Before refactoring (Complex Conditional Logic)
class Employee {
    private String type;
    private double sales;
    private double projectCompleted;
    private double salary;

    public double calculateBonus() {
        double bonus = 0;
        if (type.equals("Sales")) {
            bonus = sales * 0.1;
        } else if (type.equals("Engineer")) {
            bonus = projectCompleted * 1000;
        } else if (type.equals("Manager")) {
            bonus = salary * 0.05;
        }
        return bonus;
    }
    //...
}
```

Java
```java
// After refactoring (Using Template Method)
abstract class BonusCalculator {
```

```java
    protected double baseValue;

    public BonusCalculator(double baseValue) {
        this.baseValue = baseValue;
    }

    public double calculateBonus() {
        return calculateSpecificBonus();
    }

    protected abstract double calculateSpecificBonus();
}

class SalesBonusCalculator extends BonusCalculator {

    public SalesBonusCalculator(double sales) {
        super(sales);
    }

    @Override
    protected double calculateSpecificBonus() {
        return baseValue * 0.1;
    }
}

class EngineerBonusCalculator extends BonusCalculator {
    public EngineerBonusCalculator(double projectCompleted) {
        super(projectCompleted);
    }
    @Override
    protected double calculateSpecificBonus() {
        return baseValue * 1000;
    }
}
```

```java
class ManagerBonusCalculator extends BonusCalculator {
    public ManagerBonusCalculator(double salary) {
        super(salary);
    }
    @Override
    protected double calculateSpecificBonus() {
        return baseValue * 0.05;
    }
}

class Employee {
    private String type;
    private double sales;
    private double projectCompleted;
    private double salary;

    public double calculateBonus() {
        BonusCalculator calculator;
        if (type.equals("Sales")) {
            calculator = new SalesBonusCalculator(sales);
        } else if (type.equals("Engineer")) {
            calculator = new EngineerBonusCalculator(projectCompleted);
        } else if (type.equals("Manager")) {
            calculator = new ManagerBonusCalculator(salary);
        } else {
            throw new IllegalArgumentException("Invalid employee type");
        }
        return calculator.calculateBonus();
    }
//...
}
```

In this refactored example:

`BonusCalculator` is the abstract base class with the `calculateBonus()` template method.

`calculateSpecificBonus()` is the abstract method that is implemented by the subclasses.

`SalesBonusCalculator`, `EngineerBonusCalculator`, and `ManagerBonusCalculator` are concrete subclasses that provide the specific bonus calculation logic for each employee type.

By using the Template Method pattern, the complex conditional logic has been replaced with polymorphism, making the code much cleaner, more maintainable, and easier to extend with new employee types in the future. Now adding a new type of employee only requires creating a new subclass of `BonusCalculator` and implementing the `calculateSpecificBonus` method.

Chapter 5

Tackling Large Classes and Methods

5.1 Extract Class: Decomposing Large Classes into Smaller, Manageable Units

You're revisiting "Extract Class," and it's worth emphasizing its role in managing large classes. It's a cornerstone of good object-oriented design and crucial for keeping your codebase maintainable as it grows. As you mentioned, it's about decomposing large classes into smaller, manageable units. Let's delve deeper into this aspect.

The Problem: The "God Class"

A "God Class" (or "Blob" or "Large Class") is a class that has grown too large and complex. It typically exhibits the following characteristics:

Many Responsibilities: It tries to do too much, violating the Single Responsibility Principle.

Large Number of Methods and Fields: It has a large number of methods and fields, making it difficult to understand the class's purpose and behavior.

High Coupling: It's often highly coupled to other classes, creating a tangled web of dependencies.

Difficult to Understand and Maintain: It's hard to grasp the overall functionality of the class, making it difficult to modify or debug.

Extract Class as a Solution

Extract Class directly addresses the problems of God Classes by:

Enforcing the Single Responsibility Principle: By extracting related responsibilities into separate classes, you ensure that each class has a single, well-defined purpose.

Reducing Complexity: Breaking down a large class into smaller parts makes the overall system easier to understand and reason about.

Improving Cohesion: Each extracted class will have higher cohesion, as its elements are more closely related to each other.

Reducing Coupling: By separating responsibilities, you reduce the dependencies between classes, making the system more flexible and easier to change.

How Extract Class Helps with Manageability

Smaller Units of Code: Working with smaller classes is inherently easier. It's easier to understand the code, find the relevant parts, and make changes without affecting other parts of the system.

Improved Testability: Smaller classes are easier to test in isolation. You can write more focused unit tests that cover specific behaviors.

Increased Reusability: Smaller, more focused classes are more likely to be reusable in other parts of the system or in other projects.

Better Code Organization: The overall codebase becomes more organized and easier to navigate when large classes are decomposed into smaller, more manageable units.

Example (Revisited and Expanded)

Let's revisit the `Person` and `Address` example, expanding it to show how more responsibilities can be extracted.

Java
```java
// Before (God Class Example)
class Person {
    private String name;
    private String street;
    private String city;
    private String zipCode;
    private String phone;
    private String emergencyContactName;
    private String emergencyContactPhone;
    //... many more fields and methods relating to different aspects
of a person

    public String getFormattedAddress() { /* ... */ }
    public String getFormattedPhoneNumber(){/*...*/}

    public void sendEmergencyAlert() {
        //Logic to send an alert to the emergency contact
                    System.out.println("Sending    alert    to    "    +
emergencyContactName + " at " + emergencyContactPhone);
    }
    //... more methods
}

// After (Using Extract Class)
class Person {
    private String name;
    private Address address;
    private ContactInfo contactInfo;
    private EmergencyContact emergencyContact;
```

```java
    public Person(String name, String street, String city, String
zipCode, String phone, String emergencyContactName, String
emergencyContactPhone) {
    this.name = name;
    this.address = new Address(street, city, zipCode);
    this.contactInfo = new ContactInfo(phone);
                        this.emergencyContact    =    new
EmergencyContact(emergencyContactName,
emergencyContactPhone);
  }


          public   String   getFormattedAddress()   {   return
address.getFormattedAddress(); }
          public   String   getFormattedPhoneNumber(){   return
contactInfo.getFormattedPhoneNumber();}

  public void sendEmergencyAlert() {
    emergencyContact.sendAlert();
  }
}

class Address { /* ... */ }
class ContactInfo {
  private String phone;
  public ContactInfo(String phone){this.phone = phone;}
  public String getFormattedPhoneNumber(){/*...*/}
}
class EmergencyContact {
  private String name;
  private String phone;
  public EmergencyContact(String name, String phone){
    this.name = name;
    this.phone = phone;
  }
  public void sendAlert(){
```

```
        System.out.println("Sending alert to " + name + " at " +
phone);
    }
}
```

In this expanded example, not only is the `Address` extracted, but also `ContactInfo` and `EmergencyContact`. This makes the `Person` class much smaller and more focused on core person attributes. The responsibilities of formatting contact information and handling emergency alerts are now delegated to separate, more cohesive classes.

By consistently applying Extract Class when you encounter large, complex classes, you can significantly improve the quality and maintainability of your codebase. It's an essential technique for managing complexity in object-oriented systems.

5.2 Decompose Conditional: Making Complex Conditionals More Readable

"Decompose Conditional" is a refactoring technique that aims to make complex conditional statements (like long `if-else`chains or nested `if` statements) more readable and understandable. The core idea is to break down the complex condition and the corresponding actions into smaller, well-named methods.

The Problem: Complex Conditionals

Complex conditional logic can make code difficult to follow and understand. This is especially true when:

Long Conditions: The conditional expression itself is long and complex, involving multiple logical operators (`&&`, `||`, `!`).

Nested Conditionals: `if` statements are nested within other `if` statements, creating a deep and confusing structure.

Large Blocks of Code: The code within the `if` and `else` blocks is substantial, making it hard to see the overall flow of the logic.

How Decompose Conditional Works

Extract Condition to a Method: Extract the complex conditional expression into a separate method with a descriptive name. This makes the original `if` statement much simpler and easier to read.

Extract Then and Else Parts to Methods: Extract the code within the `if` block (the "then" part) and the code within the `else` block (the "else" part) into separate methods with descriptive names.

Replace Original Conditional with Method Calls: Replace the original conditional statement with calls to the extracted methods.

Benefits of Decompose Conditional

Improved Readability: Breaking down complex conditionals into smaller, named methods makes the code much easier to read and understand.

Increased Understandability: The names of the extracted methods clearly convey the intent of each part of the conditional logic.

Simplified Maintenance: When changes are needed, it's easier to find and modify the relevant code in smaller, more focused methods.

Reduced Complexity: Decomposing complex logic reduces the overall complexity of the code.

Example

Java
```java
// Before Refactoring (Complex Conditional)
void calculateShippingCost(Order order) {
    double shippingCost = 0;
    if ((order.getCountry().equals("US") && order.getWeight() > 10) ||
                              (order.getCountry().equals("CA")    && order.isExpressShipping())) {
        shippingCost = order.getWeight() * 2.5;
        System.out.println("Calculate US/CA shipping");
    } else {
        shippingCost = order.getWeight() * 1.5;
        System.out.println("Calculate other shipping");
    }
    System.out.println("Shipping cost " + shippingCost);
}

// After Refactoring (Decomposed Conditional)
void calculateShippingCost(Order order) {
    double shippingCost;
    if (isSpecialShippingCase(order)) {
        shippingCost = calculateSpecialShippingCost(order);
    } else {
        shippingCost = calculateRegularShippingCost(order);
    }
    System.out.println("Shipping cost " + shippingCost);
}

private boolean isSpecialShippingCase(Order order) {
    return (order.getCountry().equals("US") && order.getWeight() > 10) ||
                              (order.getCountry().equals("CA")    && order.isExpressShipping());
```

```
}

private double calculateSpecialShippingCost(Order order) {
    System.out.println("Calculate US/CA shipping");
    return order.getWeight() * 2.5;
}

private double calculateRegularShippingCost(Order order) {
    System.out.println("Calculate other shipping");
    return order.getWeight() * 1.5;
}
```

In this example:

The complex conditional expression is extracted into the `isSpecialShippingCase()` method.

The code within the `if` block is extracted into the `calculateSpecialShippingCost()` method.

The code within the `else` block is extracted into the `calculateRegularShippingCost()` method.

The `calculateShippingCost()` method is now much simpler and easier to understand. The names of the extracted methods clearly explain the logic of each part of the conditional.

When to Use Decompose Conditional

When you have a long or complex conditional expression.

When you have nested `if` statements.

When the code within the `if` or `else` blocks is substantial.

When you find it difficult to understand the overall flow of the conditional logic.

Decompose Conditional is a simple but effective technique for improving the readability and maintainability of your code. By breaking down complex conditionals into smaller, well-named methods, you can make your code much easier to understand and work with.

5.3 Replace Conditional with Polymorphism: Simplifying Complex Object Behavior

"Replace Conditional with Polymorphism" is a powerful refactoring technique that helps simplify complex conditional logic, especially when that logic is based on the type or state of an object. It leverages the power of polymorphism (the ability of an object to take on many forms) to replace complex `if-else` or `switch` statements with more elegant and maintainable code.

The Problem: Type-Based Conditionals

Often, you find code that behaves differently based on the type or state of an object. This often leads to conditional logic like this:

```Java
if (employee.getType().equals("Engineer")) {
   engineerSpecificLogic(employee);
} else if (employee.getType().equals("Manager")) {
   managerSpecificLogic(employee);
} else if (employee.getType().equals("Sales")) {
   salesSpecificLogic(employee);
} // ... and so on
```

This type of code has several drawbacks:

Difficult to Extend: Adding a new type requires modifying the existing conditional statement in multiple places.

Code Duplication: Similar logic might be repeated in different parts of the conditional statement.

Hard to Understand: The overall logic can be difficult to follow due to the nested structure.

How Replace Conditional with Polymorphism Works

Create a Hierarchy: Create a class hierarchy (either through inheritance or interfaces) where each subclass represents a different type or state.

Move Conditional Logic to Subclasses: Move the code within each branch of the conditional statement to a corresponding method in the appropriate subclass.

Declare an Abstract Method (or Interface Method): In the superclass (or interface), declare an abstract method (or interface method) with the same signature as the methods you just created in the subclasses. This method represents the polymorphic operation.

Replace Conditional with Polymorphic Call: Replace the original conditional statement with a call to the polymorphic method on the object. The runtime will then determine the correct implementation based on the object's actual type.

Benefits of Replacing Conditionals with Polymorphism

Open/Closed Principle: The code becomes open for extension (adding new types) but closed for modification (you don't have to change existing code).

Reduced Code Duplication: Common logic can be placed in the superclass, reducing redundancy.

Improved Readability: The code becomes more concise and easier to understand.

Improved Maintainability: Adding new types becomes much simpler and less error-prone.

Example

Let's revisit the employee bonus calculation example from the "Form Template Method" explanation.

```java
// Before (using if/else) - (See previous example)

//After (using Polymorphism)

abstract class Employee {
    protected double baseValue;

    public Employee(double baseValue) {
        this.baseValue = baseValue;
    }

    public abstract double calculateBonus();
}

class Engineer extends Employee {
    public Engineer(double projectCompleted) {
        super(projectCompleted);
    }

    @Override
    public double calculateBonus() {
        return baseValue * 1000;
    }
}
```

```java
class Manager extends Employee {
    public Manager(double salary) {
        super(salary);
    }

    @Override
    public double calculateBonus() {
        return baseValue * 0.05;
    }
}

class SalesPerson extends Employee {
    public SalesPerson(double sales) {
        super(sales);
    }

    @Override
    public double calculateBonus() {
        return baseValue * 0.1;
    }
}

//Usage
public class Main {
    public static void main(String[] args) {
        Employee engineer = new Engineer(5);
        Employee manager = new Manager(100000);
        Employee salesperson = new SalesPerson(500000);

                        System.out.println("Engineer   Bonus:   "   +
engineer.calculateBonus());
                        System.out.println("Manager   Bonus:   "   +
manager.calculateBonus());
```

```
            System.out.println("Salesperson    Bonus:    "    +
salesperson.calculateBonus());
    }
}
```

In this refactored example:

Employee is the abstract base class with the abstract calculateBonus() method.

Engineer, Manager, and SalesPerson are concrete subclasses that implement the calculateBonus() method according to their specific logic.

Now, the bonus calculation is handled polymorphically. The Main class doesn't need to know the specific type of employee; it simply calls calculateBonus() on the Employee object, and the correct implementation is executed at runtime. This makes the code much cleaner, more extensible, and easier to maintain.

Replace Conditional with Polymorphism is a crucial refactoring for simplifying complex object behavior and making your code more object-oriented. It promotes good design principles and makes your code more adaptable to change.

Chapter 6

Simplifying Conditional Logic

6.1 Decompose Conditional: Breaking Down Complex Conditionals

You're absolutely correct to focus on "Decompose Conditional." It's a vital technique for improving code clarity. Let's reinforce the key aspects and provide a more detailed explanation.

The Essence of Decompose Conditional

The core idea behind Decompose Conditional is to take a complex conditional statement and break it down into smaller, more manageable parts by extracting the condition, the "then" part (code executed if the condition is true), and the "else" part (code executed if the condition is false) into separate methods. This dramatically improves readability by giving each part a descriptive name, making the intent of the code much clearer.

Why Complex Conditionals are Problematic

Reduced Readability: Long, nested, or complex conditions obscure the logic. It becomes difficult to quickly understand what conditions lead to which actions.

Increased Cognitive Load: Developers have to spend more time deciphering the logic, increasing the chance of misunderstandings and errors.

Difficult to Test: Complex conditionals often have many execution paths, making it harder to write comprehensive tests.

Maintenance Headaches: When requirements change, modifying complex conditionals is risky and error-prone.

How to Decompose a Conditional: A Step-by-Step Guide

Identify the Complex Conditional: Locate the `if-else` statement or conditional expression that is causing readability issues. This is often an `if` statement with a long condition, nested `if` statements, or a `switch` statement with many cases.

Extract the Condition:

Create a new method with a name that clearly describes the condition (e.g., `isEligibleForDiscount()`, `isWithinShippingRange()`).

Move the conditional expression into this new method.

The new method should return a boolean value (true or false).

Extract the "Then" Part:

Create a new method with a name that describes the action taken when the condition is true (e.g., `applyDiscount()`, `calculateRegionalShipping()`).

Move the code within the `if` block into this new method.

Extract the "Else" Part (if it exists):

Create a new method with a name that describes the action taken when the condition is false (e.g., `applyStandardPrice()`, `calculateStandardShipping()`).

Move the code within the `else` block into this new method.

Replace the Original Conditional: Replace the original `if-else` statement with calls to the newly extracted methods.

Example (More Detailed)

Let's imagine a more complex scenario with order processing:

Java
```
// Before: Complex Conditional
void processOrder(Order order) {
    double total = order.getAmount();
    if (order.getCountry().equals("US") && order.getWeight() > 5 &&
            (order.getOrderDate().after(new Date(2024, 1, 1)) ||
order.isExpress())) {
        total *= 0.9; // Apply 10% discount for US orders over 5kg
after Jan 1st or express
        System.out.println("Applying discount");
    } else if (order.getCountry().equals("CA") && order.getWeight() >
10) {
        total *= 0.95; // Apply 5% discount for CA orders over 10kg
        System.out.println("Applying CA discount");
    }
    //... further processing
    order.setTotal(total);
}

// After: Decomposed Conditional
void processOrder(Order order) {
    double total = order.getAmount();
    if (isEligibleForUSDiscount(order)) {
        total = applyUSDiscount(total);
    } else if (isEligibleForCADiscount(order)) {
```

```java
        total = applyCADiscount(total);
    }
    //... further processing
    order.setTotal(total);
}

private boolean isEligibleForUSDiscount(Order order) {
    return order.getCountry().equals("US") && order.getWeight() > 5 &&
                (order.getOrderDate().after(new Date(2024, 1, 1)) || order.isExpress());
}

private double applyUSDiscount(double total) {
    System.out.println("Applying discount");
    return total * 0.9;
}

private boolean isEligibleForCADiscount(Order order) {
    return order.getCountry().equals("CA") && order.getWeight() > 10;
}

private double applyCADiscount(double total) {
    System.out.println("Applying CA discount");
    return total * 0.95;
}
```

Key Improvements:

Clarity: The `processOrder` method is now much easier to read. The intent of each discount rule is immediately clear from the method names.

Maintainability: If the discount rules change, you only need to modify the corresponding extracted method, not the main `processOrder` method.

Testability: Each extracted method can be easily unit tested in isolation.

Decompose Conditional is a simple yet powerful technique that significantly improves code readability and maintainability. By breaking down complex conditionals into smaller, well-named parts, you make your code easier to understand, test, and modify.

6.2 Consolidate Conditional Expression: Simplifying Multiple Conditions

"Consolidate Conditional Expression" is a refactoring technique that helps simplify code when you have multiple conditional checks that lead to the same result. Instead of having separate `if` statements or complex nested conditions, you combine them into a single conditional expression. This makes the code more concise and easier to understand.

The Problem: Scattered Conditional Logic

Sometimes, you might find code with multiple conditional checks scattered throughout a method or block of code, all leading to the same outcome. This can make the logic harder to follow and understand.

Java
```
// Before: Scattered Conditionals
double getDiscount(int age, boolean isStudent, boolean isSenior) {
    if (age < 18) {
        return 0.10; // 10% discount
    }
    if (isStudent) {
```

```
    return 0.10; // 10% discount
  }
  if (age > 65) {
    return 0.10; // 10% discount
  }
  return 0; // No discount
}
```

In this example, three separate `if` statements all result in a 10% discount. This repetition makes the code less concise and obscures the fact that these conditions represent a single discount policy.

How Consolidate Conditional Expression Works

Identify Similar Outcomes: Find multiple conditional checks that lead to the same result or action.

Combine Conditions with Logical OR: Combine the conditions using the logical OR operator (||) into a single conditional expression.

Replace Separate Conditionals: Replace the original separate conditional statements with the consolidated expression.

Benefits of Consolidating Conditional Expressions

Improved Readability: The code becomes more concise and easier to understand by grouping related conditions.

Reduced Code Duplication: Eliminates redundant code by combining multiple checks into one.

Clarified Intent: The consolidated expression clearly expresses the overall condition for the specific outcome.

Simplified Maintenance: If the condition for the outcome changes, you only need to modify it in one place.

Example (Consolidated)

Using the previous example:

Java
```
// After: Consolidated Conditional Expression
double getDiscount(int age, boolean isStudent, boolean isSenior) {
    if (age < 18 || isStudent || isSenior) { // Consolidated
        return 0.10; // 10% discount
    }
    return 0; // No discount
}
```

Now, it's immediately clear that a 10% discount is applied if the person is under 18, a student, *or* a senior.

More Complex Example with Side Effects (Handle with Care)

Sometimes, the conditions you're consolidating might have side effects (e.g., setting a flag or calling another method). In such cases, you need to be careful to preserve the original order of execution and avoid unintended consequences.

Java
```
// Before (with side effects - example is contrived to show the
point)
boolean isSpecialCustomer(Customer c) {
    if (c.hasLoyaltyCard()) {
        c.incrementLoyaltyPoints(); // Side effect
        return true;
    }
    if (c.hasMadeLargePurchase()) {
        sendNotification(c); // Side effect
```

```
        return true;
    }
    return false;
}

// After (Consolidated - but preserving side effects)
boolean isSpecialCustomer(Customer c) {
    boolean result = false;
    if (c.hasLoyaltyCard()) {
        c.incrementLoyaltyPoints(); // Side effect
        result = true;
    }
    if (c.hasMadeLargePurchase()) {
        sendNotification(c); // Side effect
        result = true;
    }
    return result;
}
```

In this case, simply combining the conditions with || would not be correct, as the side effects would only occur if the first condition was true. The refactored version ensures that both side effects occur if their respective conditions are met. Often, it's better to avoid consolidation if there are complex side effects. Consider other refactorings like "Extract Method" to encapsulate the side effects first.

When to Use Consolidate Conditional Expression

When you have multiple if statements or conditional expressions that lead to the same result.

When the conditions are relatively simple and can be easily combined with logical operators.

When you want to make the code more concise and easier to understand.

Consolidate Conditional Expression is a simple but useful technique for improving code clarity and reducing redundancy. By combining related conditions, you can make your code more expressive and easier to maintain.

6.3 Replace Nested Conditional with Guard Clauses: Improving Readability

"Replace Nested Conditional with Guard Clauses" is a refactoring technique that greatly improves the readability of code containing nested conditional statements. Nested conditionals, especially deeply nested ones, can make code difficult to follow and understand. Guard clauses offer a more linear and straightforward approach.

The Problem: Nested Conditionals (The "Arrowhead" Code)

Nested conditionals often create what's sometimes called "arrowhead code" or "pyramid of doom," where the code indents further and further to the right, making it hard to see the overall flow of logic.

Java
```
// Before: Nested Conditionals (Arrowhead Code)
void processOrder(Order order) {
    if (order != null) {
        if (order.isValid()) {
            if (order.hasItems()) {
                // Process the order
                double total = calculateTotal(order);
                sendConfirmation(order, total);
            } else {
                // Handle no items
```

```
        System.out.println("Order has no items.");
      }
    } else {
      // Handle invalid order
      System.out.println("Order is invalid.");
    }
  } else {
    // Handle null order
    System.out.println("Order is null.");
  }
}
```

This code is difficult to read because you have to mentally track multiple levels of indentation to understand the different execution paths.

What are Guard Clauses?

Guard clauses are conditional statements that exit a method early if a certain condition is met. They are typically used to check for exceptional or error conditions at the beginning of a method.

How Replace Nested Conditional with Guard Clauses Works

Identify Nested Conditionals: Locate the nested if statements that are making the code difficult to read.

Invert the Outer Condition: Invert the outermost if condition so that it checks for the opposite of the original condition.

Return Early: If the inverted condition is true, immediately return from the method. This is the "guard clause."

Repeat for Subsequent Nested Levels: Repeat steps 2 and 3 for each level of nesting.

Benefits of Using Guard Clauses

Improved Readability: The code becomes more linear and easier to follow, as you don't have to mentally track multiple levels of indentation.

Reduced Complexity: The logic is simplified by handling exceptional cases early and exiting the method.

Clarified Intent: The guard clauses clearly express the conditions under which the method should not proceed.

Reduced Nesting: Eliminates deep nesting, making the code easier to understand and maintain.

Example (Using Guard Clauses)

Let's refactor the previous example using guard clauses:

```java
Java
// After: Using Guard Clauses
void processOrder(Order order) {
    if (order == null) {
        System.out.println("Order is null.");
        return; // Guard clause
    }

    if (!order.isValid()) {
        System.out.println("Order is invalid.");
        return; // Guard clause
    }

    if (!order.hasItems()) {
        System.out.println("Order has no items.");
        return; // Guard clause
    }
```

```
    // Process the order (now at the top level)
    double total = calculateTotal(order);
    sendConfirmation(order, total);
}
```

Now, the `processOrder` method is much easier to read. The guard clauses handle the exceptional cases at the beginning, allowing the main processing logic to be at the top level, without any nesting.

When to Use Guard Clauses

When you have nested `if` statements that make the code difficult to read.

When you have conditions that represent exceptional cases or preconditions that must be met before proceeding.

When you want to simplify the control flow of a method.

When Not to Use Guard Clauses

When the "else" part of the `if` statement contains significant logic. In such cases, it might be more appropriate to keep the `if-else` structure or consider other refactoring techniques.

When the conditions are closely related and represent different aspects of the same concept. In such cases, a single `if-else-if` chain might be more appropriate.

Replace Nested Conditional with Guard Clauses is a valuable technique for improving the readability and maintainability of your code. By handling exceptional cases early and exiting the method, you can simplify the control flow and make your code much easier to understand.

Chapter 7

Working with Inheritance and Interfaces

7.1 Pull Up Method/Field: Sharing Common Behavior in Inheritance Hierarchies

"Pull Up Method/Field" is a refactoring technique used to eliminate code duplication and promote code reuse within inheritance hierarchies. When you find that multiple subclasses have identical or very similar methods or fields, it's a strong indication that this common behavior should be moved up to the superclass.

The Problem: Code Duplication in Subclasses

Code duplication is a major problem in software development. It leads to:

Increased Maintenance Costs: If a change is needed in the duplicated code, you have to make the change in multiple places, increasing the risk of errors and inconsistencies.

Reduced Readability: Duplicated code makes it harder to understand the overall design and logic of the system.

Increased Code Size: Duplication increases the size of the codebase, making it harder to manage.

When this duplication occurs across subclasses in an inheritance hierarchy, "Pull Up Method/Field" is the appropriate solution.

What is Pull Up Method/Field?

Pull Up Method: This involves moving a method from subclasses to their superclass. If the methods are identical, the process is straightforward. If they are similar but not identical, you'll need to make them consistent before pulling them up.

Pull Up Field: This involves moving a field from subclasses to their superclass. This is typically done when the field is used by the pulled-up methods or when the field represents a common attribute of the subclasses.

How Pull Up Method Works

Identify Duplicated Methods: Find methods in subclasses that have the same name, signature, and functionality (or very similar functionality).

Ensure Consistency (If Necessary): If the methods are similar but not identical, you'll need to make them consistent. This might involve:

Renaming variables or parameters: To use the same names in all methods.

Adjusting the logic slightly: To handle minor differences in behavior.

Using parameters or conditional logic: Within the pulled-up method to handle variations.

Move the Method to the Superclass: Copy the method from one of the subclasses to the superclass.

Remove Duplicated Methods from Subclasses: Delete the now-redundant methods from the subclasses.

Compile and Test: Compile the code and run your tests to ensure that the refactoring hasn't introduced any errors.

How Pull Up Field Works

Identify Duplicated Fields: Find fields in subclasses that have the same name and meaning.

Move the Field to the Superclass: Move the field declaration from the subclasses to the superclass.

Update Constructors (If Necessary): If the field is initialized in the subclasses' constructors, update the superclass constructor to handle the initialization.

Compile and Test: Compile the code and run your tests.

Example

Java

```java
// Before: Code Duplication

class Employee {

    protected String name;

    //...

}
```

```java
class Manager extends Employee {

    private int numberOfDirectReports;


    public void printDetails() {

        System.out.println("Manager: " + name);

            System.out.println("Number of Direct Reports: " +
numberOfDirectReports);

    }

}


class Engineer extends Employee {

    private String specialization;


    public void printDetails() {

        System.out.println("Engineer: " + name);

        System.out.println("Specialization: " + specialization);

    }

}


// After: Pull Up Method
class Employee {
```

```java
    protected String name;


    public void printDetails() {

        System.out.println(this.getClass().getSimpleName() + ": " +
name);

    }

}


class Manager extends Employee {

    private int numberOfDirectReports;


    @Override

    public void printDetails() {

      super.printDetails();

            System.out.println("Number of Direct Reports: " +
numberOfDirectReports);

    }

}


class Engineer extends Employee {

    private String specialization;
```

```java
@Override

public void printDetails() {

    super.printDetails();

    System.out.println("Specialization: " + specialization);

  }

}
```

In this example, the `printDetails()` method (or its core logic) was present in both `Manager` and `Engineer`. By pulling it up to the `Employee` superclass, we eliminate the duplication. Now each subclass calls the superclass method and then adds its own specific details.

When to Use Pull Up Method/Field

When you find identical or very similar methods or fields in multiple subclasses.

When you want to promote code reuse and reduce code duplication.

When you want to centralize common behavior in a single place.

Pull Up Method/Field is a valuable technique for improving the design and maintainability of inheritance hierarchies. It promotes code reuse, reduces code duplication, and makes the system easier to understand and modify.

7.2 Push Down Method/Field: Specializing Behavior in Subclasses

"Push Down Method/Field" is the inverse of "Pull Up Method/Field." It's used when a method or field in a superclass is only used by some of its subclasses, not by all of them. In such cases, it's better to move the method or field down to the specific subclasses that actually use it. This improves the clarity and focus of the superclass and prevents subclasses from inheriting unnecessary or irrelevant members.

The Problem: Inappropriate Inheritance

Sometimes, you might find that a superclass has methods or fields that are only relevant to a subset of its subclasses. This can lead to:

Bloated Superclass: The superclass becomes cluttered with members that are not universally applicable.

Confusing Inheritance Hierarchy: Subclasses inherit members that they don't use, making the inheritance relationship less clear.

Potential for Misuse: Subclasses might accidentally use inherited members that are not intended for them.

What is Push Down Method/Field?

Push Down Method: This involves moving a method from a superclass to the subclasses that use it.

Push Down Field: This involves moving a field from a superclass to the subclasses that use it.

How Push Down Method Works

Identify Methods Used by Only Some Subclasses: Determine which methods in the superclass are only used by a subset of its subclasses.

Declare the Method in the Relevant Subclasses: Declare the method in each of the subclasses that use it.

Move the Implementation: Move the implementation of the method from the superclass to each of the relevant subclasses.

Remove the Method from the Superclass: Delete the method from the superclass.

Compile and Test: Compile the code and run your tests to ensure that the refactoring hasn't introduced any errors.

How Push Down Field Works

Identify Fields Used by Only Some Subclasses: Determine which fields in the superclass are only used by a subset of its subclasses.

Declare the Field in the Relevant Subclasses: Declare the field in each of the subclasses that use it.

Remove the Field from the Superclass: Delete the field from the superclass.

Update Constructors (If Necessary): If the field was initialized in the superclass's constructor, update the relevant subclasses' constructors to handle the initialization.

Compile and Test: Compile the code and run your tests.

Example

Java

```java
// Before: Inappropriate Inheritance
class Employee {

    protected String name;

    protected int vacationDays; // Only relevant for salaried employees


    public void printDetails() {

        System.out.println("Employee: " + name);

    }


    public int getVacationDays() {

        return vacationDays;

    }


    public void setVacationDays(int vacationDays){

        this.vacationDays = vacationDays;

    }
}
```

```java
class HourlyEmployee extends Employee {

    private double hourlyRate;

    // ...

}


class SalariedEmployee extends Employee {

    private double salary;

    // ...

}


// After: Push Down Field
class Employee {

    protected String name;


    public void printDetails() {

        System.out.println("Employee: " + name);

    }
}


class HourlyEmployee extends Employee {
```

```java
    private double hourlyRate;

    // ...

}


class SalariedEmployee extends Employee {

    private double salary;

    private int vacationDays;


    public int getVacationDays() {

      return vacationDays;

    }


    public void setVacationDays(int vacationDays){

       this.vacationDays = vacationDays;

    }

    // ...

}
```

In this example, the vacationDays field was only relevant for SalariedEmployee but was present in the Employeesuperclass. By pushing it down to

`SalariedEmployee`, we make the inheritance hierarchy more accurate and prevent `HourlyEmployee` from inheriting an irrelevant field.

When to Use Push Down Method/Field

When a method or field in a superclass is only used by some of its subclasses.

When you want to make the inheritance hierarchy more accurate and focused.

When you want to prevent subclasses from inheriting unnecessary or irrelevant members.

Push Down Method/Field is a valuable technique for refining inheritance hierarchies and improving code organization. It helps to ensure that each class is responsible for the appropriate set of data and behavior, making the system easier to understand and maintain. It's the counterpart to "Pull Up Method/Field" and helps you achieve a well-structured and efficient inheritance hierarchy.

7.3 Replace Inheritance with Delegation: Promoting Composition over Inheritance

"Replace Inheritance with Delegation" is a refactoring technique that addresses situations where inheritance is being used inappropriately or is creating more problems than it solves. It promotes the principle of "composition over inheritance," which often leads to more flexible and maintainable code.

The Problem: Misuse of Inheritance

While inheritance is a powerful tool, it can be misused, leading to several problems:

Fragile Base Class Problem: Changes to the superclass can unexpectedly break subclasses, especially in deep inheritance hierarchies.

Inappropriate Inheritance: Sometimes, inheritance is used when composition would be more appropriate. This can lead to subclasses inheriting methods or fields that they don't need or that don't make sense in their context.

Tight Coupling: Inheritance creates a strong coupling between the superclass and its subclasses, making it harder to change or reuse classes independently.

What is Replace Inheritance with Delegation?

Delegation is a design pattern where an object forwards (delegates) a request to another object to perform a specific task. "Replace Inheritance with Delegation" involves replacing an inheritance relationship with a delegation relationship.

How Replace Inheritance with Delegation Works

Create a Field for the Delegate: In the original subclass, create a field that holds a reference to an instance of the original superclass (or a suitable interface). This will be the "delegate."

Initialize the Delegate: In the subclass's constructor, initialize the delegate field with an instance of the original superclass.

Delegate Methods: For each method that the subclass inherited from the superclass and wants to keep, create a corresponding method in the subclass that simply delegates the call to the delegate object.

Remove Inheritance: Remove the inheritance relationship between the subclass and the superclass.

Benefits of Replacing Inheritance with Delegation

Reduced Coupling: Delegation reduces the coupling between classes compared to inheritance. The subclass is no longer directly tied to the implementation details of the superclass.

Increased Flexibility: It's easier to change the behavior of the subclass by changing the delegate object at runtime.

Improved Reusability: The delegate class can be reused in other contexts without the constraints of inheritance.

Avoidance of Fragile Base Class Problem: Changes to the delegate class are less likely to break the delegating class.

Example

Let's imagine a Stack data structure. One way to implement a Stack is by inheriting from a List:

Java

```java
// Before: Inheritance

import java.util.ArrayList;

import java.util.List;


class Stack<T> extends ArrayList<T> {

    public void push(T item) {

        add(item);

    }
```

```java
    public T pop() {

        if (isEmpty()) {

            throw new EmptyStackException();

        }

        return remove(size() - 1);

    }

}
```

This seems convenient, but it has drawbacks. A Stack should only have push and pop operations, but by inheriting from ArrayList, it exposes all the other List methods (like add(int, E), get(int), remove(int), etc.), which are not appropriate for a Stack.

Let's refactor this using delegation:

Java

```java
// After: Delegation

import java.util.ArrayList;

import java.util.EmptyStackException;

import java.util.List;


class Stack<T> {

    private List<T> list = new ArrayList<>(); // The delegate
```

```java
    public void push(T item) {

        list.add(item); // Delegation

    }


    public T pop() {

        if (list.isEmpty()) {

            throw new EmptyStackException();

        }

        return list.remove(list.size() - 1); // Delegation

    }


    public boolean isEmpty(){

        return list.isEmpty(); //Delegation

    }


    public int size(){

        return list.size(); //Delegation

    }

}
```

Now, the `Stack` class *has-a* `List` (composition) instead of *is-a* `List` (inheritance). It only exposes the appropriate `Stack`methods, and the underlying `List` implementation is encapsulated. This is much better design.

When to Use Replace Inheritance with Delegation

When inheritance is being used primarily for code reuse and not to establish an "is-a" relationship.

When a subclass only needs to use a small subset of the superclass's methods.

When you want to avoid the fragile base class problem.

When you want to increase the flexibility and reusability of your classes.

"Replace Inheritance with Delegation" is a valuable technique for improving the design of your code and promoting better object-oriented principles. It helps you create more flexible, maintainable, and robust systems.

Chapter 8

Refactoring for Testability

8.1 Introduce Parameter Object: Simplifying Long Parameter Lists

"Introduce Parameter Object" is a refactoring technique that addresses the problem of long parameter lists in methods. When a method has too many parameters, it becomes difficult to read, understand, and use. This technique involves creating a new object to hold the parameters, thereby reducing the number of parameters passed to the method.

The Problem: Long Parameter Lists

Long parameter lists can lead to several issues:

Reduced Readability: It's hard to see at a glance what each parameter represents and how it's used.

Increased Chance of Errors: When calling the method, it's easy to pass parameters in the wrong order or with incorrect values.

Difficult to Maintain: If you need to add or remove a parameter, you have to modify all calls to the method.

Code Clutter: Long parameter lists clutter the method signature, making the code less clean.

What is Introduce Parameter Object?

This refactoring involves creating a new class (the "Parameter Object") to encapsulate a group of related parameters. Instead of passing each parameter individually to a method, you pass a single instance of the Parameter Object.

How Introduce Parameter Object Works

Identify Related Parameters: Look for groups of parameters that are logically related or that are often used together.

Create a Parameter Object Class: Create a new class to represent the group of parameters. Add fields to this class for each parameter.

Create a Constructor: Create a constructor for the Parameter Object that takes the original parameters as arguments and initializes the corresponding fields.

Modify the Method Signature: Change the method signature to accept an instance of the Parameter Object instead of the individual parameters.

Update Method Body: Inside the method body, access the parameters through the Parameter Object's fields.

Update Method Calls: Update all calls to the method to create and pass an instance of the Parameter Object.

Benefits of Introduce Parameter Object

Improved Readability: The method signature becomes much cleaner and easier to read.

Reduced Chance of Errors: Passing a single object reduces the risk of passing parameters in the wrong order.

Improved Maintainability: Adding or removing a parameter only requires modifying the Parameter Object class and not all calls to the method.

Increased Cohesion: The Parameter Object encapsulates related data, improving cohesion.

Code Clarity: It makes clear that certain parameters logically belong together.

Example

Java

```java
// Before: Long Parameter List

void createOrder(String customerName, String customerAddress, String customerPhone,

                        String orderDate, double orderTotal, String shippingAddress) {

    // ... use the parameters to create an order

    System.out.println("Customer Name: " + customerName + " Address: " + customerAddress);

}


// After: Introduce Parameter Object

class OrderDetails {

    private String customerName;

    private String customerAddress;

    private String customerPhone;

    private String orderDate;

    private double orderTotal;

    private String shippingAddress;
```

```java
        public OrderDetails(String customerName, String
customerAddress, String customerPhone, String orderDate,
double orderTotal, String shippingAddress) {

    this.customerName = customerName;

    this.customerAddress = customerAddress;

    this.customerPhone = customerPhone;

    this.orderDate = orderDate;

    this.orderTotal = orderTotal;

    this.shippingAddress = shippingAddress;

  }


    public String getCustomerName() { return customerName; }

    public String getCustomerAddress() {return customerAddress;}

    //Getters for other fields

}


void createOrder(OrderDetails orderDetails) {

    // ... use orderDetails to create an order

            System.out.println("Customer    Name:    "    +
orderDetails.getCustomerName()    +    "    Address:    "    +
orderDetails.getCustomerAddress());
```

```
}
```

```
//Usage

public class Main {

    public static void main(String[] args) {

        OrderDetails orderDetails = new OrderDetails("John Doe",
"123 Main St", "555-1212", "2024-10-27", 100.00, "456 Oak Ave");

        createOrder(orderDetails);

    }

}
```

In this example, the numerous customer and order details are encapsulated in the `OrderDetails` class. The `createOrder`method now takes a single `OrderDetails` object, making the code much cleaner.

When to Use Introduce Parameter Object

When a method has more than three or four parameters.

When a group of parameters are logically related.

When you find yourself frequently passing the same set of parameters to multiple methods.

When adding new parameters becomes cumbersome.

Introduce Parameter Object is a simple but effective way to improve the readability and maintainability of your code by simplifying long parameter lists. It makes your code cleaner, easier to understand, and less prone to errors.

8.2 Separate Query from Modifier: Improving Testability and Code Clarity

"Separate Query from Modifier" is a refactoring technique that addresses methods that both return a value (query) and change the state of an object (modifier). Such methods can be difficult to understand, test, and reason about. This refactoring aims to separate these two distinct responsibilities into separate methods.

The Problem: Combined Query and Modifier Methods

Methods that both query and modify state have several drawbacks:

Difficult to Understand: It's not immediately clear from the method signature that it both returns a value and changes the object's state. This can lead to confusion and unexpected behavior.

Hard to Test: Testing such methods requires careful setup and verification of both the returned value and the changed state. This makes tests more complex and brittle.

Side Effects: The side effects of the modification can make it harder to reason about the code and can lead to unexpected behavior in other parts of the system.

What is Separate Query from Modifier?

This refactoring involves splitting a method that both queries and modifies state into two separate methods:

Query Method: This method returns the requested value without changing the object's state. It should have a name that clearly indicates that it's a query (e.g., `get...`, `find...`, `is...`).

Modifier Method: This method changes the object's state but doesn't return a value (or returns `void`). It should have a name that clearly indicates that it's a modifier (e.g., `set...`, `update...`, `process...`).

How Separate Query from Modifier Works

Identify Methods that Both Query and Modify: Find methods that both return a value and change the object's state.

Create a Query Method: Create a new method that returns the same value as the original method but *does not*change the object's state.

Create a Modifier Method: Create a new method that performs the state modification of the original method but *does not* return a value.

Update Original Method (If Necessary): If the original method is still needed, update it to call both the query method and the modifier method separately. Usually, the original method can be deleted.

Update Callers: Update all calls to the original method to call the appropriate query or modifier method.

Benefits of Separating Query from Modifier

Improved Readability: The code becomes more self-explanatory, as the method names clearly indicate their purpose.

Improved Testability: Testing becomes much easier, as you can test the query and modifier methods separately.

Reduced Side Effects: Separating the query and modifier reduces the potential for unintended side effects.

Increased Code Clarity: The code becomes easier to understand and reason about, as the responsibilities of each method are clear.

Example

Java

```
// Before: Combined Query and Modifier

class Order {

    private int quantity;


    public int decreaseQuantity(int amount) {

        if (quantity >= amount) {

            quantity -= amount;

            return quantity;

        } else {

            return -1; // Indicate insufficient quantity

        }

    }

    public int getQuantity(){return this.quantity;}

}
```

```java
// After: Separate Query from Modifier

class Order {

    private int quantity;


    public boolean canDecreaseQuantity(int amount) {

        return quantity >= amount;

    }


    public void decreaseQuantity(int amount) {

        if (canDecreaseQuantity(amount)) {

            quantity -= amount;

        } else {

            //Handle insufficient quantity appropriately (e.g., throw an exception)

            System.out.println("Insufficient Quantity");

        }

    }


    public int getQuantity(){return this.quantity;}

}
```

```
//Usage

public class Main {

    public static void main(String[] args) {

        Order order = new Order();

        System.out.println(order.getQuantity());

        order.decreaseQuantity(5);

        System.out.println(order.getQuantity());


        if(order.canDecreaseQuantity(10)){

            order.decreaseQuantity(10);

        }

    }

}
```

In this example:

The original `decreaseQuantity()` method both decreased the quantity and returned the new quantity (or -1 to indicate an error).

The refactored code has two methods: `canDecreaseQuantity()`, a query method that checks if the quantity can be decreased, and `decreaseQuantity()`, a modifier method that actually decreases the quantity.

This separation makes the code much clearer and easier to test. You can now easily test `canDecreaseQuantity()` with various inputs without having to worry about side effects on the order's state.

When to Use Separate Query from Modifier

When a method both returns a value and changes the state of an object.

When you find it difficult to test a method due to its combined responsibilities.

When you want to improve the clarity and understandability of your code.

Separate Query from Modifier is a valuable technique for improving the quality and maintainability of your code. By separating query and modifier responsibilities, you make your code more predictable, testable, and easier to understand.

8.3 Extract Interface: Enabling Mocking and Testing Dependencies

"Extract Interface" is a refactoring technique that helps decouple code and improve testability, especially when dealing with dependencies. It involves creating an interface that defines the contract for a class, allowing you to substitute different implementations (including mocks for testing) without affecting the code that uses the interface.

The Problem: Tight Coupling and Difficult Testing

When a class directly depends on a concrete class (rather than an interface), it creates tight coupling. This makes testing difficult because:

You can't easily replace the dependency with a mock object: Mock objects are simulated objects that mimic the behavior of real objects in controlled ways, useful for isolating the unit under test.

Tests become dependent on the implementation details of the dependency: Changes to the dependency can break tests that depend on it.

Setting up test fixtures can be complex: You might need to create complex object graphs to satisfy the dependencies of the class under test.

What is Extract Interface?

This refactoring involves:

Creating a new interface: This interface declares the public methods of the class you want to decouple.

Making the original class implement the interface: This ensures that the class fulfills the contract defined by the interface.

Changing the client code to depend on the interface: This is the crucial step that decouples the client code from the specific implementation.

How Extract Interface Works

Identify the Class to Decouple: Choose the class that you want to be able to mock or substitute in tests.

Create a New Interface: Create a new interface with a descriptive name (often the original class name prefixed with `I` or suffixed with `Interface`).

Declare Public Methods in the Interface: Declare all the public methods of the class that you want to expose through the interface.

Make the Class Implement the Interface: Add `implements YourInterface` to the class declaration.

Change Client Code to Use the Interface: Find all places where the class is used and change the variable declarations and parameter types to use the interface instead of the concrete class.

Benefits of Extracting an Interface

Improved Testability: You can easily create mock implementations of the interface for testing, isolating the unit under test.

Reduced Coupling: The client code is no longer directly dependent on the concrete class, making it more flexible and easier to change.

Increased Flexibility: You can easily switch to different implementations of the interface without affecting the client code.

Improved Code Organization: Interfaces help to define clear contracts between different parts of the system.

Example

Java

```java
// Before: Tight Coupling

class EmailService {

    public void sendEmail(String to, String subject, String body) {

        // Actual email sending logic

        System.out.println("Sending email to " + to);

    }
```

```
}

class OrderProcessor {

    private EmailService emailService;

    public OrderProcessor(EmailService emailService) {

        this.emailService = emailService;

    }

    public void processOrder(Order order) {

        // ... process the order

        emailService.sendEmail(order.getCustomerEmail(), "Order
Confirmation", "Your order has been processed.");

    }

}


// After: Extract Interface

interface IEmailService {

    void sendEmail(String to, String subject, String body);

}
```

```java
class EmailService implements IEmailService {

    @Override

    public void sendEmail(String to, String subject, String body) {

        // Actual email sending logic

        System.out.println("Sending email to " + to);

    }

}


class MockEmailService implements IEmailService {

    @Override

    public void sendEmail(String to, String subject, String body) {

        // Mock implementation for testing

        System.out.println("Mock email sent to " + to);

    }

}



class OrderProcessor {

    private IEmailService emailService; // Now depends on the interface


    public OrderProcessor(IEmailService emailService) {
```

```java
        this.emailService = emailService;

    }


    public void processOrder(Order order) {

        // ... process the order

        emailService.sendEmail(order.getCustomerEmail(), "Order
Confirmation", "Your order has been processed."); // Still works!

    }

}


//Usage for testing
public class Main {

    public static void main(String[] args) {

        IEmailService emailService = new MockEmailService();

                OrderProcessor orderProcessor = new
OrderProcessor(emailService);

        Order order = new Order();

        orderProcessor.processOrder(order);

    }

}
```

In this example:

The `IEmailService` interface is extracted from the `EmailService` class.

`EmailService` now implements `IEmailService`.

`OrderProcessor` now depends on `IEmailService` instead of `EmailService`.

A `MockEmailService` was created to use in testing

Now, you can easily test `OrderProcessor` by injecting a `MockEmailService` that doesn't actually send emails, isolating the `OrderProcessor`'s logic.

When to Use Extract Interface

When you want to be able to mock a dependency for testing.

When you want to decouple code and reduce dependencies between classes.

When you anticipate needing to switch to different implementations of a dependency in the future.

When you want to define a clear contract for a class.

Extract Interface is a powerful technique for improving the testability, flexibility, and maintainability of your code. It's an essential tool for writing clean, decoupled, and testable software.

Chapter 9

Refactoring for Performance

9.1 Introduce Caching: Optimizing Repeated Computations

"Introduce Caching" is a refactoring technique used to improve performance by storing the results of expensive computations and reusing them when the same inputs occur again. Caching is particularly effective when you have computations that are:

Expensive: They take significant time or resources to compute.

Repeated: They are called multiple times with the same inputs.

Idempotent: The computation produces the same result for the same inputs, regardless of how many times it's executed.

The Problem: Performance Bottlenecks Due to Repeated Computations

Without caching, expensive computations are performed repeatedly, even if the inputs haven't changed. This can lead to significant performance bottlenecks, especially in applications with high traffic or complex calculations.

What is Introduce Caching?

This refactoring involves:

Creating a Cache: A data structure (like a `Map` or `Dictionary`) to store the results of computations. The inputs are used as keys, and the computed results are used as values.

Checking the Cache Before Computing: Before performing an expensive computation, check if the result is already present in the cache.

Storing the Result in the Cache: If the result is not in the cache, perform the computation, store the result in the cache, and then return the result.

How Introduce Caching Works

Identify Expensive Computations: Locate the computations that are causing performance bottlenecks. These are often methods that perform complex calculations, database queries, or network requests.

Create a Cache: Create a suitable data structure to store the results. A `Map` is often a good choice, where the keys are the inputs to the computation and the values are the computed results. Consider using a `ConcurrentHashMap` if the cache will be accessed by multiple threads.

Check the Cache: Before performing the computation, check if the result is already present in the cache using the inputs as keys.

Compute and Store (If Not Cached): If the result is not in the cache, perform the computation, store the result in the cache using the inputs as keys, and then return the result.

Return Cached Result (If Cached): If the result is found in the cache, return the cached result directly.

Benefits of Introducing Caching

Improved Performance: Reduces the time and resources required for repeated computations.

Reduced Latency: Improves response times for requests that involve cached computations.

Reduced Server Load: Reduces the load on servers or databases by avoiding unnecessary computations or queries.

Example

Java

```java
import java.util.HashMap;

import java.util.Map;


// Before: No Caching

class FibonacciCalculator {

    public int calculateFibonacci(int n) {

        if (n <= 1) {

            return n;

        }

        return calculateFibonacci(n - 1) + calculateFibonacci(n - 2); // Expensive recursive calls

    }

}


// After: Introduce Caching

class FibonacciCalculatorWithCache {
```

```java
private Map<Integer, Integer> cache = new HashMap<>();

public int calculateFibonacci(int n) {
    if (cache.containsKey(n)) {
        return cache.get(n); // Return cached result
    }

    int result;
    if (n <= 1) {
        result = n;
    } else {
        result = calculateFibonacci(n - 1) + calculateFibonacci(n - 2);
    }

    cache.put(n, result); // Store result in cache
    return result;

}
}

//Usage
```

```java
public class Main {

    public static void main(String[] args) {

        FibonacciCalculator calculator = new FibonacciCalculator();

        FibonacciCalculatorWithCache calculatorWithCache = new FibonacciCalculatorWithCache();

        long startTime = System.nanoTime();

        System.out.println("Fibonacci of 40 without cache: " + calculator.calculateFibonacci(40));

        long endTime = System.nanoTime();

        System.out.println("Time taken without cache: " + (endTime - startTime) / 1000000 + "ms");


        startTime = System.nanoTime();

        System.out.println("Fibonacci of 40 with cache: " + calculatorWithCache.calculateFibonacci(40));

        endTime = System.nanoTime();

        System.out.println("Time taken with cache: " + (endTime - startTime) / 1000000 + "ms");

    }

}
```

In this example, the FibonacciCalculatorWithCache class uses a Map to cache the results of the `calculateFibonacci()`method. This dramatically improves performance, especially for larger values of `n`, as the same Fibonacci numbers are not recalculated repeatedly.

When to Use Introduce Caching

When you have expensive computations that are called repeatedly with the same inputs.

When performance is a critical concern.

When the computation is idempotent (produces the same result for the same inputs).

Important Considerations

Cache Invalidation: You need to consider how to invalidate the cache when the underlying data changes. Common strategies include:

Time-based expiration: Cache entries expire after a certain period.

Event-based invalidation: Cache entries are invalidated when a specific event occurs.

Manual invalidation: Cache entries are explicitly invalidated by the application.

Cache Size: You need to consider the size of the cache and how to handle cache eviction (removing old entries) when the cache becomes full.

Concurrency: If the cache will be accessed by multiple threads, you need to use a thread-safe data structure (like `ConcurrentHashMap`) and consider appropriate synchronization mechanisms.

Introduce Caching is a powerful technique for optimizing performance. By carefully considering cache invalidation, size, and concurrency, you can effectively improve the performance of your applications.

9.2 Lazy Initialization: Deferring Initialization Until Necessary

"Lazy Initialization" is a refactoring technique that defers the creation of an object or the execution of an expensive operation until the first time it's actually needed. This can significantly improve performance, especially in cases where the object or operation is not always used.

The Problem: Eager Initialization

Eager initialization means that an object is created or an operation is performed as soon as possible, often during object creation or at the start of a program. While this is simple, it can lead to unnecessary overhead if the object or operation is not actually used.

What is Lazy Initialization?

Lazy initialization involves delaying the initialization of an object or the execution of an operation until the first time it's accessed. This can save resources and improve startup time if the object or operation is not always needed.

How Lazy Initialization Works

Declare a Variable (without initializing it): Declare the variable that will hold the object or result of the operation, but don't initialize it yet.

Check for Null (or a special "not initialized" state): In the getter method or the method where the operation is performed, check if the variable is null (or in the "not initialized" state).

Initialize on First Access: If the variable is null, initialize it (create the object or perform the operation).

Return the Value: Return the value of the variable.

Benefits of Lazy Initialization

Improved Startup Time: If an object or operation is not always needed, lazy initialization can reduce the startup time of your application.

Reduced Memory Consumption: Objects are only created when they are needed, saving memory if they are not used.

Improved Performance: Expensive operations are only performed when their results are required, avoiding unnecessary overhead.

Example

Java

```java
// Before: Eager Initialization

class Configuration {

        private DatabaseConnection connection = new DatabaseConnection(); // Eagerly initialized
```

```java
    public Configuration() {

        // ... other initialization

    }


    public DatabaseConnection getConnection() {

        return connection;

    }

}


class DatabaseConnection {

    public DatabaseConnection(){

        System.out.println("Connecting to Database");

    }

}


// After: Lazy Initialization

class ConfigurationWithLazyInit {

    private DatabaseConnection connection; // Declared but not initialized
```

```java
    public ConfigurationWithLazyInit() {

        // ... other initialization

    }


    public DatabaseConnection getConnection() {

        if (connection == null) { // Check for null

            connection = new DatabaseConnection(); // Initialize only if
needed

        }

        return connection;

    }

}


//Usage
public class Main {

    public static void main(String[] args) {

        Configuration config = new Configuration();

        config.getConnection();


        ConfigurationWithLazyInit configWithLazyInit = new
ConfigurationWithLazyInit();
```

```
configWithLazyInit.getConnection();

configWithLazyInit.getConnection();

}

}
```

In this example, the `DatabaseConnection` is only created when the `getConnection()` method is called for the first time in the `ConfigurationWithLazyInit` class. In the eager initialization example, the database connection will be established even if it is not used.

Thread Safety Considerations

If the lazy initialization will be accessed by multiple threads, you need to ensure thread safety to avoid race conditions. Here are a few ways to achieve this:

Double-Checked Locking: This is a common technique that uses a `volatile` variable and a synchronized block to ensure thread-safe lazy initialization.

Java

```
private volatile DatabaseConnection connection;


public DatabaseConnection getConnection() {

    DatabaseConnection result = connection; // Read local variable
for performance

    if (result == null) { // First check without locking
```

```java
    synchronized (this) { // Synchronize only if necessary

        result = connection;

            if (result == null) { // Double check inside synchronized
block

            connection = result = new DatabaseConnection();

        }

    }

  }

    return result;

}
```

Initialization-on-demand holder idiom: This idiom relies on the JVM's guaranteed thread-safe class initialization.

Java

```java
private static class ConnectionHolder {

        static final DatabaseConnection connection = new
DatabaseConnection();

}


public DatabaseConnection getConnection() {

    return ConnectionHolder.connection;

}
```

This is generally the preferred approach as it's simpler and more efficient.

When to Use Lazy Initialization

When the object or operation is expensive to create or perform.

When the object or operation is not always used.

When you want to improve startup time or reduce memory consumption.

When Not to Use Lazy Initialization

When the object or operation is always used. In this case, eager initialization is simpler and may even be slightly more efficient.

When thread safety is not a concern and the initialization is very simple.

Lazy Initialization is a valuable technique for optimizing performance by deferring unnecessary work. By carefully considering thread safety and using the appropriate techniques, you can effectively improve the efficiency of your applications.

9.3 Loop Optimizations: Improving Iteration Efficiency

"Loop Optimizations" encompass a set of refactoring techniques aimed at improving the performance of loops. Loops are a fundamental part of most programs, and inefficient loops can significantly impact performance, especially when dealing with large datasets. These optimizations focus on reducing unnecessary computations, minimizing overhead, and improving data access patterns within loops.

The Problem: Inefficient Loops

Inefficient loops can manifest in several ways:

Unnecessary Computations Inside the Loop: Performing calculations or operations that don't depend on the loop variable inside the loop body.

Repeatedly Accessing the Same Data: Accessing the same data structure or performing the same operation multiple times within the loop.

Inefficient Data Structures: Using data structures that are not well-suited for the type of access performed in the loop.

Unnecessary Loop Iterations: Iterating over a larger range than necessary or performing unnecessary checks within the loop.

Loop Optimization Techniques

Here are some common loop optimization techniques:

Move Invariant Code Outside the Loop: If a calculation or operation doesn't depend on the loop variable, move it outside the loop to avoid repeated execution.

Java

```
// Before

for (int i = 0; i < array.length; i++) {

    int constantValue = 10 * 5; // Invariant calculation

    array[i] = array[i] + constantValue;

}
```

// After

```
int constantValue = 10 * 5; // Moved outside the loop

for (int i = 0; i < array.length; i++) {

    array[i] = array[i] + constantValue;

}
```

Reduce Loop Overhead: Minimize the number of operations performed in the loop's control flow (e.g., the loop condition check).

Java

// Before

```
for (int i = 0; i < array.length; i++) { // array.length is recalculated each iteration

    // ...

}
```

// After

```
int length = array.length; // Calculate length once

for (int i = 0; i < length; i++) {

    // ...

}
```

Use More Efficient Data Structures: Choose data structures that are well-suited for the access patterns used in the loop. For example, using an `ArrayList` for random access is generally faster than using a `LinkedList`

Loop Unrolling: This technique involves manually replicating the loop body multiple times within the loop. This can reduce loop overhead but can also increase code size. Modern compilers often perform loop unrolling automatically.

Java

```java
// Before

for (int i = 0; i < 4; i++) {

  System.out.println(i);

}
```

```java
// After (unrolled by a factor of 2)

for (int i = 0; i < 4; i+=2) {

  System.out.println(i);

  System.out.println(i + 1);

}
```

Loop Fusion (Loop Jamming): If you have multiple loops iterating over the same data, you can sometimes combine them into a single loop.

Java

```java
// Before

for (int i = 0; i < array.length; i++) {

    array1[i] = array[i] * 2;

}

for (int i = 0; i < array.length; i++) {

    array2[i] = array[i] + 1;

}


// After

for (int i = 0; i < array.length; i++) {

    array1[i] = array[i] * 2;

    array2[i] = array[i] + 1;

}
```

Strength Reduction: Replace expensive operations (like multiplication or division) with cheaper ones (like addition or bit shifts) when possible

Java

```java
// Before

for (int i = 0; i < 10; i++) {
```

```java
    int result = i * 2;

}
```

// After

```java
for (int i = 0; i < 10; i++) {

    int result = i << 1; // Bit shift left by 1 is equivalent to multiplying
by 2

}
```

Minimize Object Creation Within Loops: Creating objects inside loops can be expensive. If possible, create objects outside the loop and reuse them.

Use Enhanced For Loops (For-Each Loops) When Appropriate: Enhanced for loops can often be more efficient than traditional for loops, especially when iterating over collections.

Java

// Before

```java
for (int i = 0; i < list.size(); i++) {

    String item = list.get(i);

    // ...

}
```

// After

```java
for (String item : list) {

    // ...

}
```

When to Use Loop Optimizations

When you have performance-critical code that involves loops.

When you are dealing with large datasets.

When profiling reveals that loops are a performance bottleneck.

Important Considerations

Premature Optimization: Don't optimize loops prematurely. Focus on writing clear and correct code first, and then optimize only if necessary.

Profiling: Use profiling tools to identify actual performance bottlenecks before applying loop optimizations.

Trade-offs: Some loop optimizations can increase code complexity. Consider the trade-offs between performance and readability. Modern compilers do a lot of these optimizations automatically so focus on clear code first and measure to see if manual optimization is needed.

By applying these loop optimization techniques judiciously, you can significantly improve the performance of your code while maintaining readability and correctness. Remember to measure the impact of your optimizations to ensure that they are actually providing a benefit.

Chapter 10

Refactoring in Practice: Strategies and Challenges

10.1 Refactoring Legacy Code: Strategies for Dealing with Untested Code

Refactoring legacy code, especially when it lacks adequate test coverage, is one of the most challenging but also most rewarding tasks in software development. Legacy code often suffers from accumulated technical debt, making it difficult to understand, maintain, and extend. The lack of tests adds a significant layer of risk, as any change could introduce unexpected bugs. Here's a breakdown of strategies for dealing with untested legacy code:

The Goal: Safely Improve the Code

The primary goal when refactoring legacy code without tests is to improve its internal structure *without* changing its external behavior. Because there are no tests to verify this, extra care must be taken.

Strategies for Refactoring Untested Legacy Code

Identify Change Points: Focus your refactoring efforts on the areas of the code that you actually need to change or understand. Don't try to refactor the entire codebase at once.

Characterization Tests (Golden Master Tests): These are crucial when dealing with untested code. The goal is to capture the *existing* behavior of the code, even if that behavior is not ideal.

How to create them:

Run the legacy code with a set of inputs.

Capture the outputs (e.g., printed text, database changes, file modifications).

Create tests that assert that the outputs remain the same after you make changes.

These tests act as a safety net, ensuring you don't unintentionally alter the existing behavior. They aren't unit tests in the traditional sense, but they are incredibly helpful for refactoring.

Sprouting Method: When you need to add new functionality to legacy code, instead of modifying the existing code directly (which is risky without tests), create a new method (a "sprout") that encapsulates the new logic. Then, call this new method from the legacy code. This minimizes the risk of breaking existing functionality.

Wrap Method: If you need to modify the behavior of an existing method but don't have tests, create a new method that wraps the original method. Implement the new behavior in the wrapper method. This allows you to test the new behavior without modifying the original method directly.

Extract Method (with Extreme Caution): Extracting methods can be beneficial for improving readability, but it's risky without tests. Make very small extractions, and after each one, manually verify that the behavior hasn't changed. If possible, add characterization tests around the extracted code before and after the extraction.

Break Dependencies: If the code has complex dependencies on other parts of the system, try to break these dependencies before refactoring. This can involve extracting interfaces or creating wrapper classes. This will make testing and refactoring individual parts of the code easier.

Change Signature: If you need to modify the signature of a method (e.g., add a parameter), do it in small steps. First, add the parameter with a default value. Then, gradually update the callers to use the new parameter. This minimizes the risk of breaking existing code.

Baby Steps: Make very small, incremental changes. After each change, compile and manually test the code to ensure that it still works. This "baby steps" approach minimizes the risk of introducing bugs and makes it easier to track down any problems that do occur.

Don't Try to Do Too Much at Once: Focus on small, targeted refactorings that address specific problems. Don't try to rewrite the entire codebase in one go.

Treat Code as Read-Only (Initially): Until you have some characterization tests in place, treat the legacy code as if it were read-only. This will force you to use techniques like Sprouting Method and Wrap Method, which are safer for untested code.

Example: Wrap Method

Java

```java
// Legacy Code (no tests)

class LegacyOrderProcessor {

    public void process(Order order) {

        // Complex, untested processing logic

        double total = order.getAmount();
```

```java
        //...lots of logic

        System.out.println("Processing order with total: " + total);

    }

}


// Refactored (using Wrap Method)

class RefactoredOrderProcessor {

    private LegacyOrderProcessor legacyProcessor;


    public   RefactoredOrderProcessor(LegacyOrderProcessor
legacyProcessor) {

        this.legacyProcessor = legacyProcessor;

    }


    public void enhancedProcess(Order order) {

        // New enhanced logic

        System.out.println("Starting Enhanced Processing");

        legacyProcessor.process(order); // Call legacy code

        System.out.println("Finishing Enhanced Processing");

    }

}
```

In this example, the new `enhancedProcess` method wraps the original `process` method, allowing you to add new behavior without directly modifying the legacy code.

Refactoring legacy code without tests is a delicate process that requires patience and discipline. By using these strategies, you can minimize the risk of introducing bugs and gradually improve the quality of your codebase. Remember to focus on small, incremental changes and to capture the existing behavior with characterization tests whenever possible.

10.2 Refactoring in Agile Environments: Integrating Refactoring into Development Cycles

Refactoring is not a one-time activity; it's an ongoing process that should be integrated into the development cycle, especially in agile environments.[1] Agile methodologies emphasize iterative development, continuous feedback, and adaptation to change.[2] Refactoring plays a crucial role in maintaining code quality and ensuring that the codebase remains adaptable throughout the project's lifecycle.[3]

Why Refactoring is Important in Agile

Responding to Changing Requirements: Agile projects are characterized by changing requirements.[4] Refactoring allows the code to evolve and adapt to these changes without becoming a tangled mess.[5]

Preventing Technical Debt: As features are added and deadlines approach, it's easy to accumulate technical debt. Refactoring helps to keep this debt under control and prevent it from becoming a major problem.[6]

Enabling Continuous Integration: Refactoring supports continuous integration by keeping the codebase clean and easy to integrate with new changes.

Improving Velocity: A clean and well-structured codebase allows developers to work more efficiently and deliver features faster.[7]

Strategies for Integrating Refactoring into Agile Development

"Boy Scout Rule": This simple but powerful rule states: "Always leave the campground cleaner than you found it." In the context of coding, this means that every time you touch a piece of code, you should try to improve it slightly.[8] This could involve renaming a variable, extracting a method, or simplifying a conditional statement.

Refactoring as Part of Every Task: Refactoring should not be a separate activity; it should be integrated into every development task. When working on a feature or fixing a bug, take the time to refactor the surrounding code if necessary.

Dedicated Refactoring Sprints (with Caution): While continuous refactoring is preferable, sometimes it might be necessary to dedicate a sprint or part of a sprint to address accumulated technical debt. However, these dedicated refactoring sprints should be planned carefully and have clear goals. Avoid large-scale rewrites during these sprints; instead, focus on targeted refactorings that address specific problems.

Use Code Reviews: Code reviews are an excellent opportunity to identify code smells and suggest refactoring improvements.[9] Encourage developers to look for opportunities to refactor during code reviews.

Automated Code Analysis Tools: Use static analysis tools to automatically detect code smells and potential problems.[10] These tools can help to identify areas that could benefit from refactoring.

Pair Programming: Pair programming can be a very effective way to refactor code.[11] When two developers work together on the same code, they can often identify opportunities for improvement that one developer might miss.

Timeboxing Refactoring: If you're concerned about refactoring taking too long, set a timebox for each refactoring task. This will help to keep the refactoring focused and prevent it from spiraling out of control.

Prioritize Refactoring Based on Value and Risk: Not all refactoring is created equal. Prioritize refactoring tasks based on the value they provide and the risk they pose. Focus on refactoring code that is frequently changed or that is critical to the system's functionality.

Make Refactoring Visible: Make sure that refactoring is visible to the entire team and to stakeholders. This can involve including refactoring tasks in sprint backlogs, discussing refactoring during sprint reviews, and tracking refactoring progress.

Example: Integrating Refactoring into a User Story

Let's say you have a user story: "As a user, I want to be able to search for products by name."

Initial Implementation: You implement the search functionality, but the code is a bit messy and has some duplicated code.

Refactoring During Implementation: While implementing the search functionality, you notice that the code for handling different search criteria is duplicated. You take a few minutes to extract a method to handle the common search logic.

Code Review: During the code review, another developer suggests renaming a variable to make it more descriptive. You make the change.

Future Iteration: In a later iteration, you need to add support for searching by category. Because the code has been refactored, it's much easier to add this new functionality without introducing new code smells.

By consistently applying these strategies, you can integrate refactoring seamlessly into your agile development process. This will help you to maintain a clean, maintainable, and adaptable codebase, allowing you to respond quickly to changing requirements and deliver high-quality software.

10.3 Common Refactoring Pitfalls and How to Avoid Them

While refactoring is a powerful tool for improving code quality, it's essential to be aware of common pitfalls that can derail your efforts. Avoiding these pitfalls will ensure that your refactoring efforts are effective and don't introduce new problems.

Common Refactoring Pitfalls and How to Avoid Them

Refactoring Without Tests: This is the most significant risk. Without a safety net of tests, you can easily introduce bugs while refactoring.

Solution: *Never* refactor without adequate test coverage. If the code is completely untested, start by writing characterization tests to capture the existing behavior.

Big-Bang Refactoring: Trying to refactor a large amount of code at once. This makes it difficult to track changes, identify errors, and revert to a previous state if necessary.

Solution: Refactor in small, incremental steps. Test after each small change to ensure that everything still works.

Refactoring Without a Clear Goal: Refactoring should have a purpose. Refactoring just for the sake of it can waste time and introduce unnecessary changes

Solution: Before starting any refactoring, define a clear goal. What problem are you trying to solve? What code smells are you trying to address?

Refactoring in the Wrong Place: Refactoring code that is not frequently changed or that is not critical to the system's functionality. This can be a waste of time and effort.

Solution: Focus your refactoring efforts on the areas of the code that are most frequently changed or that are most critical to the system's functionality.

Not Communicating Refactoring Changes: Not communicating refactoring changes to the rest of the team. This can lead to confusion and merge conflicts.

Solution: Communicate refactoring changes to the team through code reviews, commit messages, and team meetings.

Ignoring Code Reviews After Refactoring: Not performing thorough code reviews after refactoring. This can allow bugs to slip through

Solution: Always perform code reviews after refactoring to ensure that the changes are correct and don't introduce any new problems.

Not Using Refactoring Tools: Not using the refactoring tools provided by your IDE. These tools can automate many common refactoring tasks and prevent errors.

Solution: Learn to use the refactoring tools in your IDE. They can save you a lot of time and effort.

Over-Engineering: Applying complex refactoring techniques when simpler ones would suffice. This can make the code more complex than it needs to be.

Solution: Start with the simplest refactoring technique that addresses the problem. Only use more complex techniques if necessary

Refactoring Without Understanding the Code: Trying to refactor code that you don't fully understand. This is a recipe for disaster.

Solution: Before refactoring any code, make sure you understand it thoroughly. If you don't understand it, take the time to learn it first.

Not Reverting Bad Refactorings: Sometimes, even with careful planning, a refactoring can introduce problems. Not reverting these bad refactorings can lead to further complications.

Solution: If a refactoring introduces problems, don't hesitate to revert it. Use your version control system to revert to a previous working state.

Example of a Pitfall: Big-Bang Refactoring

Imagine you decide to completely rewrite a large class without any tests. You spend several days making changes, but when you finally try to integrate the changes, you discover that you've introduced several bugs. Tracking down and fixing these bugs becomes a nightmare because you made so many changes at once.

How to Avoid This:

Instead, you should have made small, incremental changes. For example, you could have started by extracting a small method, testing it, then extracting another method, testing it, and so on. This would have made it much easier to identify and fix any errors.

By being aware of these common pitfalls and following the suggested solutions, you can make your refactoring efforts much more effective and avoid introducing new problems into your codebase. Remember that refactoring is a process that requires care, discipline, and a focus on small, incremental changes.